TIRED OF LIFE?

LIFE CHANGING CHOICES AND HABITS THAT SCHOOLS SHOULD HAVE TAUGHT US TO BE HAPPY AND SUCCESSFUL

AESOP TWILIGHT

© Copyright 2020 - All rights reserved.

It is not legal to reproduce, duplicate, or transmit any part of this document in either electronic means or in printed format. Recording of this publication is strictly prohibited and any storage of this document is not allowed unless with written permission from the publisher except for the use of brief quotations in a book review.

CONTENTS

Disclaimer   v

Introduction	1
1. What is Happiness?	5
2. Learning or the Growth Mindset	30
3. Choices and Habits	46
4. Change and The Illusion of Control	68
5. A Good Life Is Built On Good Relationships	89
6. Stress	104
7. Fail More	123
8. The New Normal	139
References	157
Sources Consulted	163
Final Words	170
Tired of Life?	172

DISCLAIMER

*This book contains some strong language
that may not be suitable for all
audiences. Reader discretion is advised.*

INTRODUCTION

*A*re you happy?

Tired of the way life is? Well, I am too; understand that I am sick and tired of everything. This year has been quite a whirlwind, from the Coronavirus pandemic to the far-reaching economic changes that have resulted from it. Now, there's no job security, and instability is rampant. As if that's not enough, police brutality has been on the rise, sparking worldwide protests about the pervasive, often unspoken, systemic racism affecting many of us. Then, insert all the frightening natural disasters: bigger and more frequent forest fires, hurricanes, locust plagues, melting glaciers... Thought I was done? Not even close. These are just some of the events happening outside, we haven't even touched what's going on at home. Parents and children are strung out, worried, and stressed about the pandemic and its effects. People are dying, schools have been closed and reopened, businesses are closing, and bills are piling up.

The worst part is all these things are bringing everyone down. Nowadays, it's getting harder and harder to feel happy, confident, and secure. In 2019, we joked that the year was just awful, and we couldn't wait for it to end. But then 2020 came in and knocked the wind out of our sails. But seriously, it doesn't matter which year it is 2020 or 1890; the problem isn't the time we live in. I mean times always change. The real problem we have is the attitude and perspective we possess whenever things don't go our way, or life throws us a curveball. The question that we should be asking ourselves is: how can I be happy in times like this?

How often have you thought that if only you had X, Y, or Z, you would be happy? "I'd be happy if I had a husband/wife." "I'd be happy if I had a new job." "I'd be happy if I had a new car." "I'd be happy if I made more money." "I'd be happy if I could afford luxury items." We are always searching and looking but can't seem to find that elusive feeling of happiness. If you can relate, then congratulations, you've fallen for the biggest misconception and mental trap of all. You, like the rest of the flock, have convinced yourself that happiness comes from outside, not inside. If you looked up how to be happy, Google would be quick to give you a ton of suggestions and even recommend self-help books to read. But a lot of these books have it all wrong; in order to find happiness, one must look within.

Have you ever wondered, with all the skills and knowledge schools teach, why is it that there is no course on happiness? Before you get all excited thinking that this is just another self-help book, think again. I am not here to hold your hand and tell you that things will all magically work out. Oh no, honey! You have it all wrong. There's no easy recipe or formula for happiness; it's not a one size fits all or a magical paintbrush that will remove all the bad parts in your life. Being happy takes work, a lot of hard work. *Read that again*. Nothing is going to come easy, but once you understand the path you need to take, the results will speak for themselves.

First off, let me warn you, you mustn't take everything you read in this book so literally, some comments are just downright sarcasm. I think it would be better that way so we don't fall asleep comprehending this concept. You want to be happy. It's really quite simple. Just do it. Take control. It's all up to you.

The techniques and tips included here are designed to help you figure out happiness through the good, the bad, and the ugly. They are meant to help you keep your legs up when life pulls the rug right from under you. Because face it, in life, change is inevitable. In fact, it's pretty much a constant, so you better learn to adapt to it. Happiness in all its elusive glory takes hard work to achieve, but it has always been inside you. I'm simply here to remind you of that. The trick to finding your happiness is changing your perspective, the way you think and feel. Once you take this step, grab hold of it and watch as your life changes.

So, what are you waiting for?

1

WHAT IS HAPPINESS?

"Happiness is the meaning and the purpose of life, the whole aim, and end of human existence. Happiness depends upon ourselves."

— Aristotle

What is happiness? Do you know what true happiness is? What does it look like? Do you believe it's the same for everyone? What is the point of it all? What difference does it make in our lives? It seems like a lot to think about right off the bat, but if you are to transform your life for a happier one, you better start thinking about them a little deeper. Happiness makes up an integral part in making sense of our lives. Happier people tend to live longer, have healthier lives, make more money and do better at work. It's a chicken and egg problem, though, which comes first? Does happiness bring those kinds of things, or do those things lead us to be happier? In order to start changing your life to a happier one, you must first clearly understand what happiness is and, in turn, what it's not.

Most of us believe that we don't need a formal definition of what happiness is. And I mean, who am I to tell you what happiness is, you will know it when you feel it right? Wrong. Many of us often confuse other feelings such as pride, fun, or exhilaration as happiness. But this is a misconception that has led you, like so many others, down a mental black hole that has left you thinking the only way to be happy is to seek these feelings, often from external sources.

Before we even define happiness, let's go over some misconceptions of what happiness is.

Show me the money

True happiness is not all about money, but money can, to some extent, buy happiness. Since you've probably heard the phrase "money can't buy happiness" a million times, you may be confused. However, recent research proves that this popular saying is wrong. To a degree, we do need money to be happy, but this happiness diminishes after a certain point (Kahneman,

2010). What you need to understand is that it's not the money that's making you happy but the life satisfaction and fulfillment of basic needs coming from it.

The whole mix-up with money and happiness comes from people tying up their self-worth to financial success. This results in them engaging in more social comparisons with their peers leading to stress, anxiety, and decreased self-worth, regardless of their actual income. So it's more about how they feel and not the money they make or have. People in this society are so set on pursuing money that they don't think there's anything bad about it. However, this pursuit has adverse psychological consequences.

To be happy, you need to feel secure, and this includes financial security, which is basically freedom from worrying about life's necessities—shelter, food, and clothing. Studies show that currently we need between $60k to $95k per annum to fulfill our basic needs (Kahneman, 2010). After hitting that threshold, more income doesn't mean more happiness. In fact, it starts exhibiting diminishing returns after $75k. Income, therefore, isn't the most important contributor to how happy we are, but money does matter. It's the materialism that comes with getting money that causes unhappiness.

True happiness is not about the accumulation of material things or increasing your status. These things only bring you temporary pleasure. Surprised? You mean that new car or multimillion-dollar house isn't going to make me happy? But it has marble flooring and an infinity pool. What could be better than that? It might for about two seconds then that empty loneliness will creep back in. Can you relate?

More money more problems

We, as a society, work hard to earn more money to buy things – designer clothes, cars, houses, a trip to the Bahamas, etc. But how many lives have been broken in this pursuit of "monetary happiness?" How many times have you thought you would be happy if only you had a little more money? Take the family on vacation, kick back, and chill. However, you work such long hours you barely spend time with the family you are working so hard for. You worked so hard to purchase time for the family but, in the end, you find you don't have enough to spend it with them. What happened to all that purchased saved up time?

Picture this: you are invited to a charity event tomorrow night, so you decide to buy a new outfit. You spend the whole day shopping for the right outfit and shoes to match. I mean you have to look your best. After all that grueling work, you finally get to the event, but no one appreciates what you are wearing. Now you're sad. You tied your overall enjoyment of the event to how you will look, giving far less thought to why you are at the event.

A lot of the time, we tie our happiness to things that don't matter as much in the grand scheme, such as our looks, money, clothes, possessions, and social status. For a while, these things make us happy until they don't anymore. A lot of money can make us selfish and lonely. Cue in that miserable rich guy you just thought about now, even if it's you. Money spent the right way can buy happiness. If you spend it on others, it can lead to an increase in happiness, fostering positive relationships, and community. That's why so many billionaires have charities. They figured out that they can kill two birds with one stone; do a good deed to be happy, and get some tax relief in the process. Money spent on oneself does not change anything, it only brings in misery.

A lot of people equate individual success with making more money, increasing their personal value of money – an extrinsic reward – over other more intrinsic rewards such as relationships and community. That's why job satisfaction doesn't increase in tandem with a promotion. The correlation between income and job or life satisfaction is very small, only contributing to about five percent. Studies show that increases after a certain level in income does not affect baseline happiness (Kahneman, 2010; Jebb et al., 2018). Sure, there is a spike in happiness during the increase, but once a certain level is reached income-wise, happiness no longer increases in baseline.

Happiness is not a lack of negative emotions

Many of us are trapped in this unrealistic pursuit of happiness. We think that being truly happy means we don't have any negative feelings. Aren't they opposites? You can't possibly be happy and feel sad, right? There are two types of people who don't feel negative emotions: psychopaths and the dead. Understand, happiness is not a constant state. It's perfectly normal to have negative feelings because we are human, and we cannot suppress our nature.

Negative feelings often come from unpleasant experiences and are a part of life, and we have to experience them to have a rich, full life. They can be described as the unhappy emotions we express as a negative reaction to something or someone; if an emotion drags you down or discourages you, it is probably a negative emotion. Whenever we are happy and feel a negative emotion, we try to suppress it, which only ends up worsening the situation. While happiness can coexist with some negative emotions, misery is not part of that list. It is on the other end of the happiness spectrum. You can say misery is the polar opposite of happiness. So don't get it twisted thinking you can be happy in your misery.

Let's examine this hypothetical scenario. Tom has everything, a successful business, a lovely family, a beautiful home, and all the accolades and recognition from peers to enjoy life. Yet despite all these pleasures, he is sad. While he has momentary feelings of pleasure catching a game with his pals or enjoying the praises of his colleagues, he feels guilty, anxious, and depressed much of the time. His anxiety has become so bad that it has manifested physically as constant stomach pain and stiffness in his neck and shoulders. Poor little rich guy. He has everything anyone could ask for, why is he feeling this way?

On paper, Tom seems to have it made; however, he still can't find happiness and because he can't figure out why he feels guilty and embarrassed for having these first-world problems. So, he stuffs his feelings deep down until they manifest physically: cue his stomach pains, his stiff neck and his tense shoulders. The more he suppresses his guilt, the worse things get. Have you ever found yourself thinking, "I wish I wasn't feeling this way?" Much like Tom, you don't understand how you could be feeling both positive and negative emotions simultaneously.

While these negative emotions are unpleasant, they are fundamentally necessary for two reasons. They give us a counterpoint to positive emotions. Without these bad feelings, would positive emotions feel as good? For instance, sadness reminds us to connect with those we love, while disgust helps us reject unhealthy things. They serve an evolutionary purpose by encouraging us to act in a way that enhances our chances of survival and growth. Take fear for instance, it helps protect us from danger.

Suppressing these negative emotions turns you into a ticking time bomb. They stew and fester, and eventually, after multiplying, they explode, causing all kinds of drama. Subduing negative emotions get in the way of becoming truly happy. Rather than pretending that everything is rosy, be mindful of your feelings. If a negative feeling arises, acknowledge it, accept that that is how you feel at the time and let it go. Don't hold on thinking about why you are unhappy when you have everything you want. This negative thought loop is what drains your happiness, so get out of your head. Be honest about how you feel even when you are supposed to be happy and you are not; however, don't resign yourself to that negative feeling.

Before we get into what happiness is, let's define it. The Oxford English dictionary defines happiness as "The quality or condition of being happy." Well, okay, that's not exactly an in-depth definition. However, by taking a deeper look and defining what being happy is maybe we can finally understand how to be happy. Being happy is described as feeling or showing pleasure or satisfaction. Is that better for you? So basically, happiness is a state of feeling or showing pleasure or satisfaction. Sounds easy enough, right? All you have to do is be satisfied and just like that you will be happy. Is it really this simple and easy?

From the explanation above, there are a few takeaways we can learn about happiness:

- It is a state, not a trait that one has. This means it isn't a very long-lasting or a permanent feature of one's personality but a more volatile ever-changing state.
- Being happy is equated to feeling pleasure or satisfaction, meaning it shouldn't be confused with feelings of joy, ecstasy, bliss, or other intense feelings.
- You can feel happiness *and* negative emotions, meaning it's not always necessarily one or the other, but it can also be both.

Try and keep up now. I don't want to lose you in all this psychological stuff, Sherlock. Aren't you here because you are looking for happiness or trying to figure it out? The term happiness is often used interchangeably with subjective well-being. We often use happiness to refer to a range of positive emotions such as joy, pleasure, gratitude, and so on. However, these feelings are only a measure of how satisfied you feel with your own life and how much good or bad feelings you are experiencing at the time.

Researchers and scholars describe happiness as the experience of joy or positive well-being coupled with a sense that your life is good, significant, and worthwhile. This definition captures the nature of the positive emotions evoked by happiness and a deeper sense of meaning and purpose in life. It also suggests how these emotions and a sense of meaning reinforce one another.

With so many different takes on happiness and its deeply subjective nature, you can see why everyone is getting confused as to how they can achieve happiness themselves. However, as per some researchers, there are two main ways to approach happiness, as a global appraisal of life and all its dimensions, for instance, what you have accomplished in life. And as a recollection of your past emotional experiences, for example, by thinking of happier times.

All these definitions agree on one thing: what happiness feels like. It's being satisfied with life, being in a good mood, and feeling positive emotions. However, what these researchers have failed to agree on is the scope of happiness. What does happiness entail in its entirety? Happiness is a state marked by satisfaction and pleasure with how your current situation is.

. . .

Fun life, happy life?

In our pursuit to be happy, we engage in fun activities such as going to a party, hanging out with buddies, going to a movie, playing games, etc. By engaging in these fun activities, we believe that we are happy. How many times has someone asked you, did you have fun? Unfortunately, there is no direct correlation between a fun activity, or even a series of them, and lasting happiness (McCoy, 2016).

Disneyland claims to be the happiest place in the world. At Disneyland, you see people having fun as they go on various rides, engage in various activities, buy merchandise, allow their kids to meet and play with their favorite cartoon characters (at a price), etc. At the same time, parents watch on getting excited for them. However, the fun soon ends after you leave the park, and to have more fun, you need to go back.

Fun is what you experience during an enjoyable activity, like going to Disneyland. Similar to pleasure, it's a momentary high we try to recapture with fun activities. Unlike happiness, however, fun can be had in different ways; some of them are even self-destructive, which leads to a loss of internal happiness. Seeking fun alone won't bring your true happiness, because happiness is that good high you feel long after the fun is gone such as spending quality time with family.

. . .

Just be you

Social media is filled with 'happy' people. You know, those wannabes who look to others to get validated? In their minds, if random people like them, then they will be happy. So, they post videos, pictures, and anything they can to their adoring audience and followers and get showered with compliments such as, "You are so pretty." "I wish I had your body." "Your life is #goals." Are you guilty of this? And so begins "the gram life." You get so engrossed in your search for validation that you create a façade because you think there's no way anyone will like you for who you really are. You think that your happiness comes from the validation you get on social media, so you are willing to do anything, whatever it takes to get that high again the next time you feel you need another hit of good feelings. However, by denying who you are, you are only pushing yourself further and further toward misery, and we both know misery and happiness cannot exist in the same place. Who are you really now? Is how the world looks at you who you truly are? Honestly, aren't you tired putting up all of this to keep up with that appearance?

Happiness has very close ties with several positive feelings; let's take a look at some of them.

Pleasure versus happiness

These two terms are very similar, considering happiness is defined as a state of pleasure. Because of this, these two terms are often used interchangeably in everyday life. Why wouldn't you want to know the difference between these two states? As we stated earlier, happiness is characterized by feelings of satisfaction or contentment with your life or current situation. Pleasure, on the other hand, is a more intuitive, in-the-moment experience. It often has to do with the sensory-based feelings we get from different experiences, often dependent on external events and experiences such as making love, receiving a compliment, getting a massage, or eating good food.

What's the difference between them? While happiness is not permanent it does last longer than pleasure. Meaning happiness sticks around while pleasure comes and goes. Pleasure can add to happiness, and happiness can deepen feelings of pleasure, but the two can also be completely exclusive. For instance, you can feel happy because of something meaningful or from an engagement that has nothing to do with pleasure or a pleasurable experience. You could also derive pleasure from something, but feelings of guilt can keep you from feeling happy. That's why no matter how much food you eat, clothes you buy, or lovers you have, you just can't seem to stay happy because you keep chasing the pleasure high rather than finding longer lasting happiness.

We are a pleasure-seeking species, spending most of our time and energy seeking pleasure and avoiding pain. We hope that this will eventually make us happy, yet deep down and from our own experiences, we know that it doesn't last. With pleasurable experiences, we have to keep chasing them – eating more food, going on social media to get more compliments, earning and spending more money, having more sex – in order to feel more pleasure. As a result, we become more addicted to these external experiences, needing more and more to feel short-lived bliss.

Most philosophies, especially Indian ones, say that to achieve true happiness, one must leave materialistic desires and avoid indulging in pleasure, as it is this pleasure that causes distress too. Unlike pleasure, happiness leaves no bad aftertaste or depressing reaction, regret, or remorse. True happiness is lived repeatedly in our memories; a moment of pleasure leaves a sting, a reminder of ever-present anguish of what could or would have been...leaving a feeling of emptiness.

When seeking true happiness, a lot of us get lost in pleasurable moments thus getting stuck in a constant pleasure-seeking loop. To transform that pleasure into happiness, we need to understand these two emotions. It's okay to experience pleasure but understand that this is fleeting and even though this can enhance our happiness, this will come to pass and we should not be constantly chasing that high. Sometimes we feel guilty because we caved into our desires, but by understanding why we are feeling guilt around it and choosing not to give in, we are giving ourselves a chance to be happy. Pleasure has a nasty habit of getting into your way of finding real happiness. Don't you think it will make a difference if you gain control over your emotions and empower your awareness to know the difference between pleasure and happiness ?

Meaning versus happiness

Some think that if they find meaning in life, they would be happy. Guess what? Meaning can contribute to happiness but it's not the only thing that can make you happy. Meaning is not a temporary state that drifts in and out. There's a more comprehensive sense of purpose and a feeling of contributing to something greater than yourself. When striving for happiness, humans are just like other creatures, but the search for meaning is an integral element of what makes us human. The pursuit of happiness and meaning are two of the central motivations in life. These two elements are essential parts of achieving well-being, and while they are very distinct, they are strongly correlated, often feeding off each other. Meaning the more meaning you find in life, the happier you feel. The happier you feel, the more inspired you are to pursue even greater meaning.

However, this isn't always the case. Take parents, for instance, they often report that they are very happy to have had children, but at the same time, some of these parents score very low on measures of happiness. It seems raising children increases the meaning of their lives but decreases their happiness. Ironic isn't it? This phenomenon is known as the parenthood paradox (Rizzo, Schiffrin, and Liss, 2012). Several studies have found that happiness and meaning have a lot of common factors such as feeling connected to others, being productive, and not being bored. However, there are several differences that emerged too:

- Finding your life easy or hard, being healthy, or feeling good or lacking money is related to happiness, not meaning.
- Those who found meaning in life believe that relationships are more valuable than achievements with studies showing that good relationships contribute to happiness.
- Helping people, being consistent with your core values, and seeing yourself as a wise, creative, or productive person are all linked to meaning and can contribute to happiness.

To sum it all up, happiness has more to do with getting your needs satisfied, getting what you want, and feeling good, and finding meaning through activities such as forming a personal identity, and expressing yourself. Consciously understanding your past, present and future experiences contributes to happiness. While meaning and happiness often overlap and contribute to each other's experiences, they can be mutually exclusive.

Is happiness genetic?

Research shows that our brains are hardwired to be happy, meaning you can be happy if you know the right triggers (Sheldon & Donahue, 2017). We are born to be happy. Pause here and reflect on that. It simply means we are meant or destined to be happy. Why then are there so many unhappy people? It does make you wonder whether some of us are genetically inclined to higher levels of life satisfaction or happiness? According to a study published in the *Journal of Neuroscience* (De Neve, 2012), there is a "happiness gene" that is responsible for 33 percent of subjective life satisfaction with gene variation accounting for the margins of error. Another study showed that nearly half of one's life satisfaction is due to genetics. The other half is split between intentional activities at 40 percent and 10 percent for external events

(Lyubomirsky, Sheldon, and Schkade, 2005). Say it if you're still with me, a third to a half of me intended me to be happy and the other 40% I control. Only 10% is from the outside. Why would I choose to be unhappy then? Being able to move the happiness baseline with intentional activities increases your control on how happy you want to be or allow yourself to be.

Levels of happiness

True happiness is an inner quality, which means that no amount of clothes, money, people, or outside validation will be enough to make you truly happy. Stop sucking up to your boss or spending all that money on the latest trends; you are still going to feel hollow and empty. Ever wonder why you aren't as happy as you thought you would be despite getting all those outside pursuits you wanted so badly? I mean you put in all that work and energy to get it, you deserve to feel happy, right?

Wake up and smell the coffee, child; even if the universe handed you everything you ever wanted, you still wouldn't be truly happy. There will always be something bigger, higher you would desire...there is no end to this cycle. No amount of money, fame, power, or possessions can fill that emptiness. Happiness is a state of mind; if your mind is at peace, and you are content, you will be happy. That means that you and only you are responsible for your happiness. According to Aristotle, we can strive for happiness for its own sake. We want to strive for happiness because the act of striving will make us happier. He distinguished four levels of happiness: the Laetus, Felix, Beatitudo, and Sublime Beatitudo. Let's take a look at each one.

Level 1: Laetus – happiness derived from material objects

The first level of happiness is about sensual gratification based on something external, often material things. However, it can be quite intense and short-lived, pretty much like pleasure; it's about instant gratification. You buy a new car; you are happy showing it off to the world. You go on holiday; you take loads of pictures to show your social media fans how much fun you had. Do you get the point? This level of happiness gratifies your instinctual drive. You wanted something now you have it. You are satisfied...or are you? This instinctual drive comes from your id, a part of your human psyche that is the source of your needs, desires, wants, and impulses. For those who focus on this first level, life can quickly become shallow and lose meaning as there's a limit to the pleasure you can get from that new thing you got. Everything gets old with time.

. . .

Level 2: Felix – Ego gratification

This level of happiness is derived from comparison, being better than somebody or being admired by others. You feel this kind of happiness when you excel at something, say, sports, an exam, marry the most sought after person, or get a promotion. We all like admiration and winning; it all depends on how strong your competitive nature is. For some, it's everything; for others, it's a minor, short-lived pleasure. One thing is certain for everyone, it has an expiry date and for those who consistently seek it, this has to be renewed.

This kind of happiness is unstable because you can't win at everything, all the time. Failure usually results in unhappiness. It's unrealistic, and focusing too much on this level can cause frustration and loss of self-worth. It also results in alienating those around you because you are too self-absorbed, jealous, pessimistic, and oppressive. This happiness is linked to the ego, the part of your personality that distinguishes yourself from another.

Level 3: Beatitudo – contributive happiness

This level of happiness comes from doing good for others and making the world a better place. It's based on the basic human desire to connect with others in kindness, compassion, friendship, and help them through tough times; simply put, it's the happiness derived from love and acts of love. At this level, you move away from focusing on yourself and focus on the well-being of others. In essence, our own happiness depends in part on the happiness of others.

This love lasts longer and provides a more meaningful feeling than the first two levels. It is related to the super-ego, which always aims for perfection. Think of it as your moral compass, balancing the good and bad in your life. It guides your ego-ideals and spiritual goals – basically, your conscience. It also scrutinizes and prohibits fantasies, feelings, and actions while punishing misbehavior with guilt, shame, or remorse. The biggest limitation of this type of happiness is human imperfection. Since no one is perfect, relationships can be messy, full of disappointment, jealousy, and puts you at the risk of getting hurt, thus negatively affecting your happiness. But if you think about it, isn't that part of life?

Level 4: Sublime beatitudo – enduring and eternal happiness

This last level is achieving the ultimate, perfect happiness. But I realize that it can be difficult to describe given the subjective nature of happiness. It has to do with striking the right balance between the other levels of happiness. Think of it as transcendence. Some fulfill this desire through spirituality, philosophy, art, or science, trying to find the answers to life's biggest questions. There's no definitive definition of this level of happiness; it's something you have to figure out on your own by finding your calling.

To summarize, toward the lower levels, happiness is more immediate, sensual, and quantifiable. However, as you progress to higher levels, happiness becomes more rational, reflective, and relative. True happiness is different for each one of us...there is no one size fits all.

Where does happiness come from?

Now that you know what happiness is and conversely, what it isn't, we can look at where true happiness comes from. The answer to this is relatively easy though not so simple to attain. Happiness comes from within, and I'll keep drumming this down your throats until you get it. It's that deeper, heartfelt feeling that everything is okay. However, what is this within? When we talk about happiness coming from within, we are referring to our mindset, who we are, and not how we feel, per se.

Happiness is an internal choice. It comes from what you talk about, think about, and your behaviors. Which all coincidentally are tied to our mindset. You can create happiness within your life, even when it seems impossible. In my not so humble opinion, it's not the things around you that are making you happy, you are happy because of your outlook on things. Aristotle defined happiness as the meaning and purpose of life. For him, it referred to a long-term pattern of action rather than a singular emotion. Basically, the sum of your character and habits acquired over the years.

At some point, you unconsciously decided that things or people would make you happy and did they? We all have things we believe will make us happier. Some we choose unconsciously, while others are beliefs that we learned from school, our parents, or other people. And somewhere down the line, we convinced ourselves that these things are a vital component for us to feel truly happy. Eventually, you discover that they don't fill you with happiness the way you thought they would, and you are left feeling sad and miserable.

It stands to reason that, if we change our outlook then we can be happy. Sounds easy enough; all you've got to do is change how you think, then it's all tea parties and daisies. Wake up, numbnuts, nothing is easy. Change is, in fact, a painful, grueling experience, but without pain, there's no gain. Regardless of how you are feeling, the way you perceive your life is what determines your happiness. If you are overwhelmed by bad thoughts and assumptions such as, you don't have enough money, or your job is horrible, then you will be unhappy. Flip that around, with a positive mindset; you can still remain happy even in bad times. What have we discovered so far? Your perception is your reality. Wouldn't changing your perception make all the difference?

Why wouldn't you want to change? According to research, the average person has 12,000-60,000 or even 80,000 thoughts per day. Of these, 80 percent are negative, and 95 percent are repetitive. Already, most of the thoughts you will have today are negative. Then, you decide, "You know what? Let me consciously add more negativity to the mix." The result is a brooding mass of misery where you are angry with yourself and everyone else.

Your happiness is dependent on several factors including the type of personality you have, the good and bad emotions you feel, your attitude toward physical health, social class, wealth, relatedness and attachments, time, place, goals, and self-belief. Researchers have also proved that performing kind acts has powerful ripple effects on our subjective well being and overall happiness (Stoerkel, 2020). Seems like they were onto something here because when it comes to happiness Antoine de Saint-Exupéry said it best, "what's essential is often invisible to the naked eye." It's not money or material things, but feelings such as love, sacrifice, service, and affection for those you love that bring about real happiness. That's why, despite experiencing negative emotions, we can still be happy. There is no singular formula for happiness, no one standard blueprint you can follow. The path to finding true happiness is different for every individual. Recognize that there are different kinds of happiness to suit different kinds of people in the world. Happiness, and you can get this tattooed on your forehead, is as diverse and unique as humans.

2

LEARNING OR THE GROWTH MINDSET

*"Your thoughts are incredibly powerful.
Choose yours wisely."*

— Dr. Joe Dispenza

Ultimately, that's the goal, right? You want to change. But, obviously, that is easier said than done. Do you ever think, "why do I still have the same behaviors even while saying I want to change?" "If happiness comes from within, what's stopping me from making new positive behaviors habits?" "How can I become the happier person I have always wanted to be?"

Well, you aren't alone. Everyone struggles with change, especially long-term change. It comes down to our thinking and how we see things. Our mind is split between the conscious mind, that's aware of everything happening at the moment and the subconscious mind, a powerhouse where the memories and habits we have learned over the years are ingrained in us. You know that alcohol, smoking, and junk food is bad for you, yet you continue to consume them. You just can't pass on a juicy burger and some fries. It's like chewing on razors, willingly, and hoping not to get cut. But why am I like this, you ask? It's your subconscious; that part of your brain that controls your habits and only cares about instant gratification and self-preservation.

The instant gratification part is pretty clear; you are chasing that pleasure high that makes you think that these things make you happy. But what about the self-preservation part? This is the main reason why your subconscious mind doesn't like change. Over the years, the many experiences and memories you have had developed a fixed belief system of how it should react and think at any given time based on unfiltered thought; think of it as your default setting. Any challenge to this belief set will almost provoke a reaction of anger or denial.

Because of the fixed belief system that only cares about instant gratification and self-preservation, we often end up sabotaging ourselves whenever we try to change. Take money for instance. We pretty much do anything to have it: lie, cheat, and even steal because we believe that it will make us happy. The subconscious mind doesn't know right from wrong. That's why it's hard to convince yourself that all that hard work you are putting in to get more money won't give you the happiness you crave deep inside.

By nature, your subconscious is singular. It doesn't exist in a world of duality as we do. It does not agonize between good and bad. It has no moral compass or the capability to discern right from wrong. This makes it impossible for the choice your subconscious mind makes to be wrong; that is why we still engage in things we know are bad for us, such as junk food, drugs, your ex, etc.

Let's get back to the point, lest we forget why you are here: what this has to do with your happiness. We have discovered that there are two parts of you, the caring moral human and the habitual, instinct-driven creature that follows the same path every time, good or bad. To attain true happiness, these two parts must work together for the good of the whole. At this point, there's no internal conflict; you don't feel guilty about being happy or enjoying yourself even when others say you shouldn't. Happiness isn't all about what happens to you but rather how you choose to respond. That's why it's called happiness, not "happeness."

Why it's so hard to change habits

Your subconscious mind doesn't care about you or

your happiness any more than it cares about getting its next fix; it's like a crackhead high on habits. That's why so many feelings, such as pleasure, fun, achievement, success, and meaning, are mistaken for happiness. To truly be happy, you need to change your outlook. However, that's like trying to get a computer program to do something it's not programmed for. You'll need to program it how you want it. Changing our behavior is a self-engineering feat with few equals. I don't mean the short bursts like New Year's resolutions, but rather long-term sustained change.

If you had a penny for the times you have sworn you'll start working out, you'd be swimming in money. You probably stick with it for a couple of weeks, then one day, you just don't feel like doing it anymore. My point, whether the change involves habits, dependencies, diet, or anything else, changing behavior is the hardest part of the journey. *Read that again.* Changing your behavior is the *hardest* part of the journey.

Thankfully, this is a well-researched subject, and a lot is known about why changing habits and behaviors is so hard. Here are some of the reasons:

1. Negative emotions are our biggest motivators – I can see why you would think that strong negative emotions such as revenge, shame, guilt, fear, and regret would be great catalyzers for behavioral change.

They often burn hot and fast, injecting much-needed fuel to spur change. However, the opposite is true. While negative emotions may trigger you to think about everything you are doing wrong, they make horrible catalyzers. Behavioral studies show that the least consistent change strategies are hinged on fear, shame, or regret (Harvard Health Publishing, 2012). Real change needs a positive platform as a foundation. If you want to change, you need to find positive, self-edifying reasons to change.

2. Thinking fallacies trap us – change is hard and can be overwhelming. The frustration it causes tends to foster an all or nothing mentality: "If I don't change, that's it. I never will." If you are up-to-date on your mental biases and distortions, then you know that this all-or-nothing type of thinking is way up there. Add this on top of convincing yourself that happiness is found externally, and you have no control over it, then you are trapped in a no-win situation. These fallacies lower your odds of sustaining change even with the proper motivation. Think of all the gym memberships in January spurred by New Year's resolutions

to be healthier. By March, they have all dwindled to nothing because, after a week of working out, most people call it quits saying it's too hard. To make lasting change, you have to remove these thinking fallacies and purge any other thinking errors while we are at it.

3. We try to do everything at once – behavioral change is a big undertaking no matter the behavior, and it's practically impossible to take it all on at once. You have to start somewhere, with measurable actions. Wanting to be happy is a noble cause, but it's too big and too vague. You need small and specific actionable steps on how to be happier. Instead of saying you want to start working out. Take a short 30-minute walk. Each specific action you take contributes to your behavioral change. Engaging these little steps over time, results in a cumulative change. To achieve change, say to lose a certain amount of weight, we need specific and realistic goals and performance targets to measure our progress.

We love multitasking, and it's easy to think, well if I can commit to changing one habit long term why not go for more? But trying to take on multiple behaviors is a surefire way to sabotage yourself. The resources needed to make change happen, such as motivation, attention, or self-control, are limited. Taking on multiple behaviors places unrealistic demands on these resources and dooms your efforts from the start. You forget that other areas in your life require the same resources, so even one more additional behavioral change commitment is a deal-breaker.

1. Not having the right tools – to change a flat tire, you need a jack point, lug wrench, and a spare tire. Why should changing our behavior be any different? These tools, devices, or techniques provide reliable go-tos to help support sustainable change. To lose weight, exercise and a diet change are needed. Changing our diet requires, at the least, that you get more information about healthier eating habits and make an action plan. The same goes for happiness; you need a set of tools to support your change in the long run. These can include cultivating gratitude through being thankful for all the gifts you have each day. Meditating on your life for about 10 minutes a day. Finding ways to reduce and cope with stress, doing acts of services such as helping others out, etc.
2. Underestimating the process – change is

not singular; it's a combination of things. Sustainable change doesn't happen without a process that integrates all the pieces involved. Our life lessons are no different, so there is no running from the work. It's easy to lie to yourself and believe that it would be simple. That's why so many people believe that happiness comes from outside. It shifts the workload to the external factors. But nothing about behavioral change is simple. It is a tough process-oriented challenge. To move that happiness dial even a little requires a lot of blood and sweat.

3. We forget about failure – if you are going to try something, there's a 50/50 chance that you will fail, and with change, it's no different. Failing is part of the process and it's one of life's sturdiest truths. How many times did you get hurt before you learned how to ride a bicycle or skate? But you want to change habits forged out of years of experiences and memories just like that? You already know that change is hard, what makes you think you will nail it on the first try? Setting such unrealistic goals is what feeds into the all-or-nothing mentality we discussed earlier. Talk about self-sabotage.

Failure is not all bad; it reveals what deserves more attention and energy in the next try. All change techniques and models factor in failure as a step, not the end, or an excuse to stop. You got that?

4. We are not committed – last but not least, if you don't commit to accomplishing this behavioral change, it will not happen. How could it? You can't half-ass something and then magically expect it to work out. You need a commitment device, something that firmly ensures that you follow through with what you plan on doing, and how you will do it. Commitment devices help you avoid akrasia or acting against your best interests like you do when you procrastinate. They are a way for self aware individuals such as yourself, who know what they want, to modify their motivations to overcome unwanted habits. An extreme example of this would be of Han Xin (Dubner, Stephen J. and Levitt, Stephen D., 2007), a general in ancient China that had his soldiers positioned with their backs to a river whenever they fought so they had no choice but to fight the enemy head-on. Find the Han Xin of your journey to true happiness.

Now that it's all starting to come together, you understand why working out or sticking to a diet has never really stuck with you. You've been pushing a boulder up a hill, but this is only part of it. Let's take a look at the mind, the other half of the change equation.

The growing mindset vs. the fixed mindset

People are not born; they are made, meaning you are a culmination of your past experiences borne out of our choices. These, in turn, shape your thoughts, beliefs, and habits which influence your mindset. Can what you believe impact your success or failure at something? Well, according to Carol Dweck, a psychologist at Stanford and overall go-to guru on all things pertaining to the growth mindset, your beliefs play an integral role in what you want and whether you will achieve it (Dweck, 2007). She has discovered that your mindset plays a vital role in determining your success rate.

So what is a mindset?

A mindset refers to your disposition about your abilities, whether you believe that qualities such as intelligence, or talent, are fixed or changeable traits. Your mindset plays a vital role in whether you succeed or not. There are two kinds of mindsets: the growth mindset and the fixed mindset. Those with a fixed mindset think that their abilities are inborn, fixed, and unchangeable, pretty much set in stone. Those with a growth mindset on the flip side believe that these abilities can be learned or developed and strengthened through commitment and hard work.

In her research, Dr. Dweck argues that people with a growth mindset are more likely to succeed than those with a fixed mindset since they believe that their abilities are capable of developing over time (Dweck, 2007). The growth mindset is one of the foundations of positive psychology, which posits that you can learn optimism and develop your strengths and grow your happiness. This growth mindset sets out a formula for success and happiness in life by being the driving force behind motivation and achievement. For example, if a child wants to get smarter, then learning is the goal. And if they put a bit of effort into it by spending time learning and working hard at it, they will ultimately achieve their goal of getting smarter. Easy, right? With such a mindset, we can understand that being happier takes effort, good learning, and persistence. Even though you are not as happy as you would like to be, you believe that you can be happier if you work towards it.

Along with a growth mindset, you must understand that your brain can grow and change even become stronger. Our ability to learn is an amazing thing, this can help us break out of the many happiness traps we have convinced ourselves will lead to happiness. Getting out of the achievement trap to find solace in the act of doing is what happiness is all about. This belief boosts confidence and improves learning. Research shows that our brains are plastic, not the kind of plastic that litters the world, but rather in reference to its malleability.

In neuroscience, this is referred to as neuroplasticity, which alludes to the mind's ability to change, grow, and shape itself through the act of doing. Essentially, what you put in is what you get out. So basically, neuroplasticity is your brain's ability to restructure itself based on repetitive practices. With focus and practice, the brain can change; it can grow new cells and neural pathways and even strengthen new learning.

Why mindsets matter

In subsequent studies, Dr. Dweck found that mindsets significantly impacted one's motivation, effort, and approach to challenges (Dweck, 2007). Your mindset affects the cognitive, affective, and behavioral features linked to your beliefs about the malleability of your intelligence. This list shows how different mindsets lead to different behavior.

	Fixed Mindset:	**Growth Mindset:**
	Believes that abilities such as intelligence are static, inborn or set in stone. Basically, you have it, or you don't.	Believes that abilities such as intelligence can be developed. They are not necessarily inborn or set in stone. Basically if you are not good at it, you can learn it.
	Having the mindset leads to a desire to look smart and a tendency to react, as shown below,	Having the mindset leads to a desire to learn and a tendency to react, as shown below,
Challenges	Avoids Challenges	Embraces Challenges
Obstacles	Gives up easily. It's all-of-nothing	Keeps going even through failure and setbacks
Effort	Sees effort as fruitless or not worth it. It is the gateway to their inadequacies	Views effort and hardwok as the path to mastery
Criticism	Views criticism negetively and as an affort and ignores any useful feedback it may contain	Takes criticism positively and learns from it
The success of others	Feels threatend by the success of others	Feels happy for others and finds lesson and inspiration from them
End result	They plateau early on in life and realize less than their full potential.	They reach higher levels of achievement, getting closer and closer to their full potential.
	This line of thought conforms to a deterministic view of the world.	All this gives them a greater sense of free will as they can do anything they set their minds to.

Your mindset changes what you strive for and what you see as success. It alters the definition, significance, and impact of failure while changing the deepest meaning of effort. On one mindset, failure is about setbacks, getting a bad grade, losing a promotion. It means you are not clever or talented enough to reach for the things you value, and thus you aren't fulfilling your potential. Here effort is also a bad thing. It also shows you aren't talented or smart enough, because if you were, you wouldn't need to put in this much effort. However, failure isn't the end of the world, but merely a bump on the road and effort is what makes you smart and talented. By changing your mindset, you are essentially entering a new world and seeing things in a different way.

Seeing the characteristics of these two mindsets, why wouldn't you want to change? With a fixed mindset, you have resigned yourself to fate. To you, happiness is something you have no control over, you are either happy or not. And I bet you are not most of the time. If your mindset does not shift from fixed to growth, then all this knowledge is lost on you. So stop right here, the rest of the stuff I'm going to talk about will be of little benefit to you. *Bye!*

We have all read books that say success is all about being your best self. But, it's important to note that failure is an important learning tool. Failure is an opportunity, not a condemnation, but rather effort is the key to success. But those with fixed mindsets can't put any of this into practice because their belief in fixed traits is telling them something completely different. To them, success is about being more gifted than others, that failure does measure you and your level of effort, and hard work is for those who can't make it on talent.

You can see the flawed logic here, right?

Dr. Joe Dispenza believes that your personality creates your personal reality. Want to venture a guess on what your personality is based on? Yes, your mindset. Being happier is all about changing your perception. This change in perception puts you on the path to creating new habits and behaviors. By changing our mindset and adapting our personality to create and impact new results, we can change our reality.

When we foster a growth mindset, we are actually learning how to change our brains to make them better at learning and being happier. There are certain areas in your life that are so fixed that you might not be aware that there's another way. A growth mindset builds a passion for learning rather than a hunger for approval and gives you the fluidity you need to take on life and discover the wonders waiting out there.

Those with a growth mindset are not deterred by challenges or failure; in fact, they welcome them because they don't actually see themselves failing in those situations. Why waste time demonstrating how great you are over and over again? Why spend all that time and effort hiding your deficiencies? So what if you have a great life and you are not truly happy? Where's the crime there? Why do you look for friends, partners, or things to boost your self-esteem rather than seek out those who will challenge and grow you? The passion for putting yourself out there and sticking to it even when things are going bad is the hallmark of the growth mindset. It's what allows you to thrive even in the most challenging of tasks such as changing habits.

In a fixed mindset, everything is instant, perfect, and has perpetual compatibility. Like it's meant to be, riding off into a sunset and living happily ever after. Therein lies the problem. You expect everything to happen automatically, like magic, sort of how it happened for Cinderella, who was saved from her miserable life by her prince or like what happened to Aladdin, who found the magic lamp that granted all his wishes.

After considering everything, a reasonable person can conclude that a growth mindset is not only the best option but a necessity in your difficult journey to finding true happiness. It will help frame failure as a learning opportunity and spur passionate efforts towards your overall goal of being happier. After all, it's the effort that matters. Shifting your mindset sounds easy, but as I said before, nothing is easy. It takes practice and effort.

3

CHOICES AND HABITS

If you are to undergo any real attempt to change yourself, then we are going to need to take a good, long look at your habits. We develop habits to help us navigate the world, and we can be aware of them or not. Thanks to the basal ganglia, these behaviors are automatic, much like blinking, and so they help us get our daily needs met more efficiently. However, because these habits are so deeply ingrained in us, even if a habit is bad, it can be difficult to break. Knowing how habits are formed is the first step if any real effort is to be made to dismantle and replace them.

Habits can be good or bad. Having a puff first thing in the morning, taking a run, going to the gym, hard work, reading, writing, meditation, dishonesty, escapism, or buckling your seatbelt are all examples of habits. Most of us have habits that we don't even give any attention to. For example, we brush our teeth at night while on autopilot. This is a beneficial habit, so we don't need to worry much about it, but what about all those negative habits that are also automatic or on autopilot?

Your life today is a summation of your habits. How happy or unhappy you are, whether you are in shape or not, and how successful or unsuccessful you are. What you repeatedly do, or spend time thinking about every day, ultimately forms your personality, beliefs, and person. Think about that for a minute. It's not all your spouse's fault you're not happy at home, or your boss' fault you hate your job; it's all you.

Humans have habits because they are efficient; you can perform useful behavior without wasting time and energy deliberating on what to do. This quick-and-efficient response tendency also has its downsides, especially when bad habits hijack it. Aren't procrastination, telling lies, and deceiving also habits?

HABIT FORMATION

The neuroscience

Recent advancements in neuroscience show that our brains are more malleable than we thought (Fuchs and Flügge, 2014). While looking into neuroplasticity, researchers discovered how the connectivity between neurons can change with experiences. With practice, these neural networks can form new connections, strengthen existing ones and insulate them, speeding up impulse transmission. What all the science is saying is that we can increase the growth of these neural connections with the actions we take. But I'm getting ahead of myself here. What do neurons have to do with habits?

MIT researchers identified that if neurons fire at the beginning of specific behavior, then it becomes a habit (MIT, 2019). They fire at the start of new behavior and subside after it occurs, then fire again once it's finished. Over time patterns in the brain known as neural pathways and behavior form and become automatic. That's why breaking a habit is so difficult because it is literally hardwired in your brain.

To better understand how habits are formed, let's take a look at what goes on in the brain. In the forebrain specifically, an area known as the basal ganglia controls voluntary movement. It also plays a crucial role in the formation of habits, whether good or bad, as well as emotional expression. It helps us form habits so they can become automatic, freeing up space in your conscious brain to take on day-to-day activities. These automatic habits include brushing your teeth or driving and even breathing. However, it's also responsible for the formation of unwanted or unhealthy habits such as anxiety, addictions, eating disorders, and so on. Like I said before, your subconscious mind has no moral compass. It forms habits, both good and bad.

A habit can be described as an instinctive response to a specific situation, acquired as a result of learning and repetition. A simplistic form of learning or a behavioral change caused by experience. When a behavior develops to a point, it becomes highly automatic and doesn't require conscious attention; it's a habit. Many dominant problems we have in life are preventable. Take, for instance, heart disease. Adopting health-promoting behaviors such as eating healthier or working out can significantly improve one's quality of life, both mentally, physically and reduce the chances of getting heart disease. Why not do the same with happiness?

Many times habits are mistaken for routines, with the terms often used interchangeably. While both involve repeated behavior, a routine is not necessarily carried out in response to a desire or craving like a habit is. You routinely clean the dishes or work out without feeling a desire to do because you feel you have to do them, with or without a reward. Where habits are behaviors that require no conscious thought, routines require a high degree of intentionality and effort.

People develop habits in the course of pursuing various goals by associating certain cues with behavioral responses that help them meet the goal or obtain a reward. While driving to a certain place, say the beach, you follow particular routes and road markers to get there. Over time, thoughts of the behavior and the behavior itself are triggered by these cues. The same can be said about happiness. What you repeatedly do and spend time thinking about whenever you are happy will be the cues that will trigger future happiness.

Habits are formed physiologically and psychologically. When an act is repeated, various neurons are connected, and a neural pathway is formed. From a psychological standpoint, when a stimulus is related, and a specific response is elicited, the connection between them is strengthened, eventually bringing on learning. So psychologically, habits are acquired dispositions born from any learning experience, repeated until it is firmly retained.

The habit loop, a term coined by Charles Duhigg in *The Power of Habit* (Duhigg, 2014), describes the various elements that produce habits. These elements are cue, behavior, and reward. Think of them as the steps or backbone of habit formation, and your brain goes through them in the same order each time. Breaking down habits to their fundamental parts can help you understand what it is, how it works, and how to change it.

Step 1: The cue

The cue consists of two parts: the trigger and the craving. The trigger initiates a specific behavior in your brain. It's the information that predicts a reward. Take smokers, for instance, their trigger is usually stress. Whenever they feel anxious, that's their cue to smoke a cigarette. We use a lot of our time learning cues that predict secondary rewards such as money, power, fame, status, approval, love, praise, friendship, or personal satisfaction. Your mind is continually on the lookout for external and internal cues of where rewards are located. Since it is the first indication that you are close to a reward, it naturally leads to a craving. Cravings can be thought of as the second part of the cue step. They are the motivating force behind every habit. In our smoker example, the relief they feel whether physiologically or psychologically from smoking leads to the craving of that relief. This becomes their motivation and desire. Devoid of some motivation or desire, you have no reason to act.

Let's be clear, what you crave is not the habit itself but the change of state it brings. You don't crave junk food; you crave the feeling that eating brings, that delicious satisfaction of biting into a juicy burger. You don't crave smoking; you are after the relief it provides. You don't actually want to brush your teeth; you want that feeling of fresh breath and a clean mouth. You don't want to watch TV; you want the entertainment it brings. You get the gist? Every craving is linked to a desire to change your internal state.

Cravings are different for each one of us. Theoretically, anything can trigger a craving; but, we are not all motivated by the same cues. For an avid gambler, a slot machines' whirring and chimes are a potent trigger that sparks an intense desire to play. However, for those who rarely gamble, they are just background noises. Until they are interpreted, triggers are meaningless; it's the thoughts, feelings, and emotions that you attach when you sense them that transforms them into cravings.

Step 2: The response or behavior

The response or behavior is the actual habit you form in response to the cues. It can either be a thought or an action. Whether a behavior occurs will depend on how motivated you are and the work or effort associated with it. If a particular response requires more physical or mental work than you are willing to do, guess what? You won't do it. How you respond to a cue depends on your ability. A habit can only occur if you are capable of it. Take dunking a basketball, for example, if you can't jump high enough, then tough luck, you can't dunk. This doesn't apply to happiness, though; we are all capable of happiness, so you can't use this as an excuse not to be happy.

STEP 3: THE REWARD

Lastly, after the response comes the reward, the end goal of every habit. The trigger is about noticing the reward, the craving is about wanting the reward, and the response is about getting the reward. We chase rewards for two purposes. First, they satisfy our cravings by providing benefits of their own. Food gives you the energy you need. A promotion brings you that feeling you get from more money and respect. Working out gets you in shape, improving your health, and your dating life. However, a more immediate perk of rewards is satisfying your craving to win, improving your status, or fulfilling your desire to eat. They temporarily deliver contentment and relief from our cravings.

Secondly, rewards teach us the actions worth remembering. Since your brain is a reward detector, as you go about your daily life, it constantly monitors which actions satisfy your desires and bring you pleasure. Pleasure and frustration are part of the feedback mechanism that help the brain discern useful and useless actions. Rewards are the last step in the habit loop; they close the habit cycle.

If any behavior falls short in any of these steps, it doesn't become a habit. If you take out the cue, your habit never triggers; reduce the craving and you lack the motivation to do it. Make the behavior difficult and you won't have the ability to do it. If the reward fails to satisfy your craving, there's no reason to repeat it. What I want you to understand is a habit needs all three steps to form. Without all three, the behavior won't occur or be repeated.

These stages of habit formation create an endless cycle that runs every minute of every day. This system is constantly searching the environment, trying to predict what will happen, trying out different responses, and learning from the results. The cue triggers a craving, which motivates a response which yields a reward, that satisfies the said craving, which now becomes associated with the triggering cue. Together they form a neurological loop, cue-craving-response-reward that ultimately creates automatic habits. This means they form neural pathways in this pattern for every behavior.

Habit formation can more simply be split into two phases: the problem and solution phase. The problem phase includes the trigger and craving, when you realize something needs to change, and the solution phase with the response and reward, where you take action to achieve your desired goal. Understand that all behavior is driven by a desire to solve a problem, and habits are how you do this. You wake, you want to feel more alert, so you drink a cup of coffee. Drinking coffee satisfies your craving to be alert, so it becomes associated with waking up.

When you are all grown up, you barely notice the habits running your life. You never give another thought to how you always change into more comfortable clothes after getting home. These decades of mental programming eventually turn into automatic thought patterns and actions.

Creating new habits

Old habits are a pain to shake off, and developing new ones is even harder. However, it is possible. So how do you create new habits? Well, we have already gone through step one, understanding how habits are formed.

"If you know the enemy and know yourself, you need not fear the result of a hundred battles. If you know yourself but not the enemy, for every victory gained, you will also suffer a defeat. If you know neither the enemy nor yourself, you will succumb in every battle." – Sun Tzu, *The Art of War*

By understanding how a habit is formed, you are gaining insight into your enemy (habits) and yourself.

Just like Sun Tzu said, you stand a better chance at winning when you know your enemy, and make no mistake, this is a war; this is a war for your happiness, and right now, the bad habits keeping you from living a happier life are winning. We can then turn them into practical frameworks that you can use to change your habits and even eliminate bad ones. Think of each stage as a building block that influences your behavior. With the blocks calibrated correctly, creating good habits will be easier. To create a good habit, make the cue obvious, the craving attractive, the response easy, and the reward satisfying.

Given the cue-dependent automatic nature of habits, channeling these fundamental laws of habit formation is the key to creating new habits. Adding the habit formation components to any attempt at real behavioral change can help shield new behaviors from motivational lapses and increase their long-term sustainability. For some behavior, one instance is enough to attain the desired result. Taking a single vacation can help you relax faster and drastically reduce your stress levels. However, for most behavior, repetitive action is required to achieve meaningful outcomes. To achieve long term happiness, you have to deliberately cultivate a culture of gratitude and service. In such instances, behavioral change must be viewed as a long-term process divided into two stages: initiation and maintenance.

This distinction is important as a lot of people fail at attaining long-term change despite having the capability, opportunity, and motivation to initiate the change. They often lapse back into old behavior patterns after a drop in motivation. New Year's resolutions, anyone? This change can be attributed to a drop in motivation after initial experiences of the action. See how people love running from hard work? Others overestimate the positive outcomes of the action and feel disappointed when the outcomes fall short of their expectations or fail to factor in the negative outcomes. Alternatively, a newly acquired behavior can lose its value and become deprioritized over time. What I'm trying to say is, a loss in motivation can permanently derail any successful attempts at behavioral change.

Since habits form from what you do rather than what you think, here are some simple hacks to help you create good habits.

1. **Define your context** – context here refers to your immediate environment, except yourself. This includes where you live, the people you are with, what time of day it is, and even the actions you perform. Just as a gourmet chef sets up their kitchen to make it easier to cook, you need to organize your environment to make it easier for you to do the same thing repeatedly. We don't often

realize how much our environment and the pressures around us drive our actions. If you want, let's say, to stop binge eating, remove the temptation, the food and the cue – hunger. Eat tiny healthy portions more frequently during the day so that you are not starving by the time you get to your meal.

2. **Repeat, repeat, repeat** – a behavior will only turn into a habit through conscious repetition. This consistency increases its accessibility and prominence, so when you are in a similar context, the habit automatically commences. Logically, you may be wondering just how long it takes to build a habit. Well, popular opinion says it only takes 21 days to create a habit. *Wrong*! Studies have proven that it takes anywhere between 6 to 9 months to build a habit effectively. And you thought you'd be done in a month! With the increased timeline, you run the risk of losing momentum along the way and finding the habit less rewarding. Since happiness is something you want to structure into your life, don't you think it's worth all the work?

3. **Up the rewards** – with an organized context and repetition to jumpstart your habit

building, you need to sweeten the pot if you are to actually succeed and get these habits to operate on their own. The rewards have to be bigger and better than what you would normally expect. When it comes to behavioral change, intrinsic motivation, the internal force that pushes you, is invaluable. However, incentives come in real handy at this point. They can help with habit building by motivating you, even more, to engage in the desired behavior.

Why you may ask? Because unexpected rewards spur the release of dopamine, a feel-good hormone, that etches the circumstances of the rewarding experience into memory, making you more likely to repeat the behavior. This creates an energy that invigorates you to pursue actions that have positive outcomes and achieve your happiness goals. If you want to work out because it boosts your moods, but you hate going to the gym, you are not going to get in shape unless you add something such as listening to music while working out to entice you into doing it. The more fun it is, the more likely you are to turn it into a habit.

If you still have trouble building healthy habits, you can try:

- **Stacking** – rather than making a big change, start small. Try forming a habit by taking advantage of an existing behavior to cue a new one. For instance, if you have some medication to take after breakfast, placing it on the table when you eat (morning habit) automatically reminds you to take it after breakfast. To build long term, happier habits, try stacking them onto other habits. If you are searching for things to be grateful for, give compliments, and if you get some back, practice appreciating the person giving you the compliment. This way you will have something to be always grateful for.
- **Swapping** – it pretty much means exactly that; swap out a habit you already have with something similar. If you want to stop drinking sodas, try switching to bottled tea. Since the packaging is the same, and you carry and use it just like a soda, the substitution will be easier to accept. Rather than frowning, smile, because it's a frown turned upside down!

Training your brain for happiness

Current neuroscience theories state that our brains are organized to reflect what we know about our environment, our relationships, the things we own, the places we have been, and all our experiences (Bransford, et al, 2000). All these things, even our behaviors, and actions are tattooed onto our brain matter. However, our brains' neuroplasticity lets us remodel and change these neural pathways to produce the behaviors and habits we want. Contrary to popular belief, you have more control over your brain than what you assume you have. Think of all the people who have changed their lives to happier ones, don't you want that?

Our genes can provide us with about 50 percent of our happiness. Food, shelter, and safety provide another 10 percent. This leaves 40 percent entirely up to us. Training ourselves to be more self-aware and through various exercises to change how we think to be happier, optimistic, and resilient to negative emotions, we can effectively change the neural connections and train our brains for happiness. When we learn how to feel good, our physical health, psychological well-being, and functioning all improve. To achieve this change, there are some habits or cognitive distortions we have to let go of. These include:

- **Perfectionism** – first off, we can never be perfect, so the pursuit of perfection pits you against your own nature. How could you be happy? Perfectionism is often mistaken for meticulousness, which involves appropriate and tangible expectations. Perfectionism, on the other hand, involves unrealistic levels of expectations and intangible goals. Perfectionists often have the all-or-nothing type of thinking, seeing things in black and white, rather than in the colorful splendor that is reality. When things don't go their way or are not to their standards, they view themselves as failures, making them failures. I mean, seriously, why take on all that? Trying to attain perfection only creates problems. Is it even worth it? That said, even though attaining perfection is nearly impossible we don't need to abandon it completely but rather look at this pursuit more of a journey rather than the final destination and every action we do that yields results as a learning opportunity.

- **Comparisons** – in life, it's an inevitability that you will compare yourself with others at some point. You will often find yourself lacking, triggering feelings of anger, low self-esteem, and inadequacy. That's why when you see other people living happy lives, you feel envious…you feel bad. That said, you can have what's known as a healthy social comparison. This isn't about seeing yourself as a failure but using it to find out what you admire in others and imitating those admirable qualities or even improving on them. The best comparison you can make, however, is with yourself. Take a look at your past and see where you were. Are you at a better place now than you were in the past? What can you do to further improve yourself?

- **Maximizing** – have you ever found yourself not going for something because you are waiting for a better deal? Have you ever bought something and think, I bet I could have gotten a better deal on this? Maximizers search for better deals even when they have already gotten what they need. It is very important to distinguish between what we want and what we need. Oftentimes, we are better off with just getting what we need rather than getting what we want. Maximizers lose out on the opportunities to be present in their lives and enjoy the good moments they have. They also have very little gratitude because you can't be thankful if you aren't satisfied, right?

- **Materialism** – you've heard it countless times, attaching your happiness to material things is a dangerous game to play. What will happen if you lose your job and you can't sustain that lifestyle? What then?
- **Overgeneralization** – this refers to holding every experience you had to be true and applicable to every other experience every time. For example, your last relationship ended badly, so apply that experience to other blossoming relationships and conclude you will never have a good one. The thing with overgeneralization is it views failure as the end and closes you off to trying things again. Remember, this journey to happiness is hard, and failing is part of it. However, if you hold onto these failures and say that you will fail every time you try, you most definitely will because you won't even try and that's the sure-fire way to ensure your failure 100%. Would the odds be better if instead of 100% guaranteeing failure by not trying to at least try with a chance of 10% success or even 1%? That's still better than 0% when you don't even try.
- **Downplaying the good** – finding ways to downplay your positive moments like they don't count, saying it was luck or you failed

less than others. Acknowledge your successes.
- **Skewing your reality** – assuming as true that what you are feeling is always a representation of reality. "I made a mistake during my presentation. Everyone must think I am a fool." Really?
- **Jumping to negative conclusions** – making leaps of negative conclusions without any evidence to support your claim. "I know something is going to go wrong." You act like you are suddenly psychic and know what will happen, or like you can read minds, "I know they will hate me." How do you know for sure?
- **Letting past mistakes define you** – defining yourself based on your past mistakes or perceived lack of skills. For instance, saying you are not smart enough because you failed at something before or thinking that you could never achieve the same success as others, and refusing to try things out because you think you will fail.

As you can see, all these distortions or flaws in thinking are all telltale signs of a fixed mindset.

Our brains are already wired for happiness and positive connections with others. Despite how we are genetically hardwired, we can still learn new behaviors or modify existing ones. Though the concept of mental rehearsal – repeatedly imagining doing the action – the neural circuits in our brains rewire themselves to reflect our intentions. A study (Vyas et al., 2018) asked people to just mentally rehearse one-handed finger exercises for at least two hours per day. They did these mental exercises for five days and demonstrated the same neural changes as those who physically performed the same exercises. To put it plainly, when you are truly focused and single-minded on a particular task, your brain cannot differentiate between the internal and external world. If you can mentally rehearse being happy, your brain will create the neural networks to reflect your intentions.

This allows you to change your neural wiring without doing the action physically first and thus giving you a shot to form the habit. By changing your mind, independent of environmental cues or cravings, and holding this ideal steadfastly, your brain will function as if the action has already happened. In other words, your brain will act as a radar system for happiness triggers because it has already experienced happiness. Now, as you go about your life and face the same circumstances that negatively affected your happiness, you now have the appropriate neural pathways in place to allow you to change the circumstances in your favor. Think of it this way, the device and software updates have been made, so now you can handle any challenge thrown your way. Where you would have insisted on things being perfect, you can now rest easy knowing things are up to a certain standard even though they aren't perfect.

To make change stick, we need to repeat behaviors that work consistently in our minds and through action. Focus your mind on your desire to be happy, then discipline the body to act in alignment with this goal. Despite the environment, you can achieve sustained happiness because your mind and body are one. This mental exercise gives you a better chance of turning your new behaviors into habits. It's all about choice...make the conscious effort to choose to be happy .

4

CHANGE AND THE ILLUSION OF CONTROL

"There is no life without change. The real tragedy is that we are always fearful of change and resist it vehemently."

— DEBASISH MRIDHA

Imagine you are rock climbing with friends when out of nowhere you lose your footing and slip. A moment ago, you were thrilled thinking you would do this, it's not so bad; now, all you can think about is, "What if I fall?" Even though you know the harness is there and secure, you still panic.

Imagine another hypothetical. After ten years of working at your job, you've just recklessly abandoned ship. You finally quit! You actually took that chance and left the security of your job. However, after the adrenaline rush is over, you are gripped with cold, raw fear.

My question is, what are you actually afraid of? What's the primary focus of your fear? In the first example, will you slip and fall even though the harness is secure? Or will you not find another job in the second example? What you are really afraid of isn't the climb itself but the uncertainty that the situation brought. It's not losing the job that frightens you but how it has thrown your future into uncertainty. You had already made plans for the future, so where will you get the money to finance them?

We all experience some level of fear when it comes to change; that's why comfort zones exist. Rather than quit to get a more satisfying job or venture out on your own, you stay at the miserable workplace for years. You were confident you could make the climb and soon enough you have adjusted well in your job and this has made you comfortable. You are now familiar with your work and making friends at work. Nothing could go wrong you think...or could it? You believed your shoes wouldn't slip and the gear would keep you safe. However, once you slipped, you went into panic mode. Suddenly in your mind, the path ahead was filled with slippery moss and other obstacles that could cause you to fall, which interestingly enough, was not there before you slipped.

Don't worry, though; you are not alone in this

thinking. Billions of people all over the world are all paralyzed by the same fear of change especially when life throws you a curveball. While it would be easier and simpler to blame your lack of willpower and call you cowardly for not embracing the fear and taking change head-on, it's your mind that is to blame for making you run and hide in the face of change. Neuroscience has shown that in our brains, uncertainty feels similar to failure (Grupe and Nitschke, 2013). That's why so many of us avoid change because of how uncomfortable and painful the feelings can be.

But what exactly are we afraid of? Is it the particular act of failing or the uncertainty of not knowing what lies ahead? Let's hypothetically say you won the lottery and the options are, A – you could receive $40,000 a week up to the time you get all of your $10,000,000 winnings or option B – you get $1,000,000 in one lump sum payment. Which one would you pick? Even though both outcomes would lead to a win, if you are merely afraid of not knowing what lies ahead, you will be drawn into taking the safe option, B. Even though you are accepting a $9,000,000 loss, you would rather do that and make sure you secure your winnings than take the risk of the company closing or something happening that might prevent you from collecting your whole winnings. What if I just collected $100,000 before the company went bankrupt or I died? Had I accepted the $1,000,000, I'm ahead

Tired of Life?

$900,000 now. This way, you know exactly what you are getting now. What about the $9,000,000 you lost by not taking option A? You are more scared of losing $900,000 than losing $9,000,000?

We fear change because we are afraid of losing what is associated with that change. For instance, you would rather stay in a crappy marriage because you don't want to lose the years you put into it. You don't want to leave that miserable job because you don't want to start at a new one, even if it's better than your current one. Our aversion to uncertainty and loss is so bad it even causes logic to fly out of the window. Remember the climb? Even though you know the path ahead is safe, and your gear is secure, you are still afraid of climbing higher because you don't know whether you will slip again or not.

This is what makes change so scary – how our mind perceives it. Whenever something changes in your life, even little things like the type of creamer you put in your coffee, it can trigger anxiety, stress, and even pain. Bigger changes such as changing jobs, leaving a toxic relationship, or going against the grain can cause panic attacks, depression, fatigue, more pain, and loads of stress. If we don't know how something will turn out, we would rather not try it because we fear the outcome could be bad. But aren't we just getting ahead of ourselves here?

Understand that this fear is an illusion. That

doesn't mean you won't experience fear, far from it. When you are afraid, you may feel everything from panic attacks to physical symptoms. What you must understand is the driving factor behind your fear of change is almost always false. It is often based on limiting beliefs and habits. It's not valid in terms of the probability of it coming to fruition, meaning that bad outcomes you keep dreading may or may not happen. Sometimes we even create a bigger scenario in our head than what it would really be. Fear has a very interesting acronym: False Evidence Appearing Real. When I talk of fear, I'm not only referring to that spine chilling terror that grips you sometimes but to any negative based thoughts, feelings, or emotions. This can include worry, doubt, anger, jealousy, anxiety, etc.

If our thoughts are anything to go by, there is no question that we are fear-aligned, since 80 percent of our thoughts are negative – big surprise there – and 95 percent of thoughts are repetitive, which means that there's a 95 percent chance that you will have the same negative thoughts today, tomorrow, and even two months from now. That's not even the best part. Most of the fear-based thoughts you worry about *never ever happen*. That's right, 85 percent of those fearsome, worrisome thoughts never occur. Of the 15 percent that do happen, research has found that people often find that they can handle the challenges a lot better than they expected if they, as Nike would put it, "JUST DO IT".

In short, we spend our lives worrying over the exact same thoughts we worried about yesterday, and what's crazy is that they may never even come to fruition. Yogis have a name for this; they refer to it as the "monkey mind." I call it *madness*.

This irrationality can be more accurately attributed to the ego. You know that little voice in your head that claims it's a voice of reason? At its core is a false perception that you are separate from everything and, therefore, limited in a way. Eckhart Tolle defines it as a dysfunctional relationship with the present (Tolle, 2005). In that, the ego is always either in the past (living in regret) or looking at the future (worrying), never in the present, never accepting things as they simply are. When ego comes in the way, we lose our ability to sense the connections that exist all around us. We live in the past or worry about the future; fear becomes our daily bread.

Why do we fear change?

An experiment was conducted where a group of people was asked to look at the same painting. The first group was told it was from 1905, while the second group was told it was from 2005. Those that thought the painting was from 1905 thought it was more aesthetically pleasing than those who thought it was from 2005 (Grupe and Nitschke, 2013). This is because we like that which has been around for a while. It's pretty much why we hate change and new things. Curious, isn't it? However, this runs much deeper than that. We fear change because of the uncertainty and loss it brings. We would rather be unhappy than risk being unsure of things?

Your brain is even wired to avoid uncertainty. To it, uncertainty registers much like an error, which causes discomfort, and it needs to be corrected so we can feel comfortable again. Our brains are designed to find peace in knowing. For many people, change means uncertainty. When we don't know what will happen, we make up scenarios and worry about them rather than focus on what we can do with the actual situation. We have a hard time moving on when something such as a relationship comes to an end because our fear of failure feeds into our fear of change. We start thinking about what people are going to say about us, so we stay in the relationship and the vicious cycle of unhappiness continues.

Here are more reasons why you probably fear change:

- **Loss** – well, we have mentioned this before. A big chunk of why you fear change is because of what you risk losing. You could be thinking, what am I being asked to give up? Do I have to let go of my marriage, job, or wealth? Some see a change in job titles as a threat to their self-worth, their status, and their self-esteem. Even little things such as moving desk positions can make you unhappy if it means losing a window, wall, or access to the common area, or the perception that you have been downgraded. To overcome this sense of loss, take time to absorb the change. Focus on the positive but be frank with yourself about the situation.

- **Confusion** – if you don't understand the reason behind change, it creates confusion, and you will tend to resist it. This is because of the uncertainty caused by the change. It pushes us out of our comfort zone, and boy, do we hate that. Our habits and routines help us feel secure; without them, we feel lost and confused. To remove this fear, make sure you understand why this change is necessary, how it will help and why things cannot carry on as they are.
- **Incompetence** – you might be fearful of change because you think you are not capable of doing what you are hoping to do or don't have the skills to take on such a

task. You could be thinking, will I look stupid? Will my skills be not enough? Rather than figure out this concern, you would rather fight the change.

- **It requires work** – well, there's no two ways about this. *Change requires work. A lot of work.* It takes time, dedication, and perseverance. You have to break old habits, build new ones, and that results in an increased workload. This can make change feel like a burden. However, you must recognize that change comes with obstacles. Don't take everything on at once; pace yourself. Prioritize what you need to do and acknowledge the hard work you have put in.
- **Losing control** – lastly, change can make you feel like the rug is being pulled right from under you because of that feeling of losing control. The larger the change, the more you feel powerless in all of it. No one likes feeling that way. You are going to grasp onto every last straw you can find to maintain this outside illusion of control. We believe that if we have control over our lives, things won't be as scary. Remember, the mind finds comfort in knowing, so if you have control over things, you know

everything will play out the way you expect it to or will it?

Overcoming the fear of change is difficult, like untangling your shoelaces while running away from a serial killer difficult. And, if change makes you nervous, know that you are not alone. However, you won't find happiness unless you are willing to take that dive off the deep end into, you guessed it, uncertainty. Being happy will require you to do things that might leave you knee-deep in uncertainty. Take quitting your job. You don't know what your future holds, and that's scary; however, is it better to stay in your crappy job?

WHAT IS THE OUTSIDE ILLUSION OF CONTROL?
One of the things that keeps us from change, especially positive change, is our impression that controlling the outside will lead to happiness. We think that we can get rid of fear by controlling the situation. Stephen R. Covey, in his book, *The 7 Habits of Highly Effective People*, talked about this concept. Think of yourself as existing in a free space. Now, draw a circle. Let's call it the circle of concern. Within it lies everything you are concerned about in your life from your job, health, family, finances, politics, the environment, stocks, other people's decisions, and moods, etc. This circle encompasses everything that matters to you, so

whatever is outside should be of little or no concern to you (Covey, 2004).

If you think about the things within your concern circle, you will quickly realize that they are divided into two groups: those within and those out of your control. For instance, you might be worried about the health of a loved one or inflation; however, there's very little you can solely do to control those. Identify the things that are within your control. Draw another circle, and put the things you can control there. This is your circle of control. It consists of things within your control, such as your happiness, health, finances, etc. Now draw another circle between your circle of concern and control. This is the circle of influence; it consists of things that are out of your control but that you can influence. For instance, you can influence loved ones to eat healthier and work out, positively impacting their overall health.

This exercise is a great way to reevaluate yourself and your priorities. It helps build resilience by helping you identify what you can and can't control. For those concerns that you can't control, stop worrying about them. You cannot affect the weather, so why should it have a say in your happiness? What you have control over is bringing an umbrella or wearing a jacket. This exercise helps you become more self-aware of the things in your life. Once what you can't control is out of the way, you are left with your circle of influence.

More often than not, you will realize that you influence a lot more than you think. *You are not powerless.*

This simple realization can change your attitude and response to these things. The simple act of acknowledging the influence you have can create relief. It gives you the confidence to talk about and face your fears. This openness lets you address the concerns you have over the changes you have to make and identify potential stressors. Let me dumb it down for you; once you know the power you wield, your circle of control increases. This reduces the uncertainty that comes with change, and so you are more open to it.

That said, you cannot control what's in your circle of influence, so don't put all your hopes in it. Understand that you can only influence things in this circle, not control them; *This is key.* Once you understand that you can only affect the behavior of others and not control it then you know your happiness is no longer hinged on their opinion of you. You now know control of others is an illusion. You can not control how they will think or react to you. It won't matter whether your social media followers think you are beautiful or not because you know you are and nothing they say or think should change that. Knowing people are free to react or think however they want will lead to the realization that at best all you can "hope" for is to influence how they think or react to you. In the end, they will still do what they think and feel they should do and that's not because of any fault of yours.

Your attitudes, body language, choices, and behavior all fall within your circle of influence. And while it can be argued that some things are done unconsciously, as a result of our habits. We can also say that when we are self-aware, we control and make conscious choices. Reactive people often blame others for their behaviors and tend to use their personality as a crutch or shield. In comparison, proactive people accept responsibility for their behavior and do their best to live within their control circle. Do these two types of people sound familiar? Well, they should. They are representations of the growth and fixed mindsets we talked about earlier on. Do you see how much power your mind has? How much power do you have?

Therefore, the solution to overcome the fear of change is using small, consistent actions within your circle of control and to a lesser degree to your circle of influence. It's all about focus. What you focus on is what you will put your energy into. By narrowing your focus to the things within your circle of control and influence, you can stop worrying over things you have no control over. You can easily get trapped in the victim mindset of thinking you have no control over something, thus setting yourself up for failure by stressing over things you cannot control. You have no control over other people's decisions, so whatever they chose to do or say, that's on them. What you can control are your behaviors and words and consequently your happiness.

Reality and Happiness

"We apply reality from within. The world is our perception of the world. So what other people think of you, famous or not, is an independent construct taking place in their brain, and we shouldn't worry too much about it." – Russell Brand, *Revolution*.

I can assume that you have thought about what others think of you at some point, and because of that, I can assume that you have thought. The act of thinking is a revolutionary thing that few creatures on this earth can do. René Descartes was onto something when he came up with, "I think, therefore I am." So tell me, when did it become what others think is who you are? Is what your Facebook friends commenting on your post your reality? If they say you are beautiful, tall, thin, fat or ugly, is that all true? Does it influence what you think of yourself? Does it make you upset? How do you discern between opinion and reality?

Reality is defined as the state of things as they are instead of the idealistic notions we have of them. What this means is how we see the world isn't really how it is. What we perceive as reality is an internal reconstruction of the mind. A study conducted by Robert Lanza proved this theory, which stems from the scientific understanding of particles and how they behave when observed versus how they behave when they think they are not being watched (Lanza and Berman, 2010) (talk about loco).

He stated that our understanding that a candle flame is yellow is actually a mental illusion. Unobserved the candle has no yellowness. These qualities are acquired after interaction with a conscious being. There's nothing inherently visual about the flame. It's when the electromagnetic impulses it produces react with the cells in our retinas that we see a yellow flame. Other animals might see the flame as gray. The difference is because our brain reacts with a complex matrix of neurons.

How is this linked to happiness? We all have varying viewpoints of the world, which color our view of it, meaning we can put varying weight behind things. How you see things is different from how I see them, which is also different from how they actually are. See how confusing all this is?

Despite what you might think, we are surprisingly inept at predicting our happiness. Newlyweds tend to think that their happiness levels will rise or stay the same over the first four years. In reality, the opposite is true. Their happiness tends to diminish over the four years. Lottery winners, those lucky bas*****, even after getting all that money return to the same happiness levels they had before winning, sometimes even lower with the passing of time. We believe that that stellar job, perfect relationship, or ideal bank account will effectively boost our happiness. And they do, however, this boost is surprisingly short-lived.

We are wealthier than ever but unhappier. We are more prosperous than ever, but we are also more depressed and less satisfied. We have developed faster transport, but rather than be happy about achieving that, we have found more ways to preoccupy the time we saved. It seems that despite an increase in technological advancement, there's no corresponding increase in overall life satisfaction and happiness. In pursuit of happiness, we set several expectations which we confused for happiness goals and thus pursued the wrong thing. This is referred to as the expectation gap, when our expectations exceed our reality.

THE EXPECTATION GAP

Pip, from Charles Dickens' *Great Expectations* is a great example of the expectation gap. He inherited some money from a secret benefactor and viewed this acquisition of wealth and promotion in stature as a stepping stone to marrying the girl of his dreams. However, he ultimately learns that money was not part of life's grand plan. He realized that he had taken so many important relationships and gifts in his life for granted. He expected that getting money would make him happier; however, his expectations robbed him of fully appreciating his reality.

When our expectations exceed reality, we don't fully appreciate what we have because we expect more or compare it to what we could have. We tend to savor our lives less and color our enjoyment of it based on our expectations. We, therefore, don't get to actually enjoy things as we should. How many times have you focused on getting something else that you forgot to enjoy what you had? You're so intent on getting more money for your family that you barely spend whatever you already earn with them. Your expectations of greater things make you feel like what you have isn't really great when others would kill to have what you have. Simply put, we are often unhappy because our expectations of reality exceed our experiences of it.

Our expectations are formed by three things: our imagination, those around us, and our past. These, in turn, form the different types of expectations we have. The imagination gap occurs when your imagination exceeds your reality. When we select what products to buy or where to travel, we often pick from various options. But how do we make this decision? By going with the one we think or imagine will be the best. This allows you to maximize your choice at a given price. To do otherwise would be going with an option you didn't think was as good in the first place, which would be counterintuitive. Therein lies the problem. The very act of selecting the option you think is the best and will bring you happiness undermines your happiness because it sets you up for an expectation much bigger than reality. What this means is that when we then experience reality, it doesn't live up to our expectations, leading to disappointment.

Technology only seems to make this worse. It has made unrealistic things appear real, even things that weren't on the happiness scale before, seem as though they are actually possible. We Photoshop things in, airbrush things out, and digitally enhance photos all to create this illusion. This changes our view on whatever choices we have to make, and we come up with fantasies reality simply cannot live up to. Technology skews our vision, distorts reality, and makes the unreal seem real. Our imagination differs from reality, setting us up for disappointment when we finally get to experience it. That's why a vacation is never as good as the pictures make it appear.

When we travel, we are happiest when we stumble upon unexpected things or discover things on our own, devoid of preconceived notions based on pictures or videos taken of the place. What makes this worse is selection bias. The content on many search engines or social media is ranked based on views or likes. You are more likely to see an enhanced picture if it has more views or likes. This makes us think of the ideal images as normal and average, and so we set our imaginary expectations with that as a baseline. After experiencing reality, we become disappointed. So we are stuck in this loop of having our expectations raised only for them to be shattered devastatingly. When the limited resources of reality meet our minds' limitless expanses, we are disappointed and experience unhappiness. Expectations and disappointment are, therefore, irrevocably linked. We have become a society of people who always imagine different and better outcomes for themselves, but our imagination cannot be satisfied, leaving us perpetually disappointed.

The second gap is the interpersonal gap, where we compare our reality with that of others. Simply put, we judge ourselves based on the surrounding experiences. Your pain is someone's gain, and someone's pain is your gain. If you have $100,000 in a poor neighborhood, you'll feel rich; however, you'll feel poor if you are in a wealthy neighborhood. If you get a small raise while others around you get a higher pay raise, you will be disappointed. This doesn't apply to income only, but even to appearance. Research shows that we are happier when we are with worse looking people because we are seen as objectively better looking. So, the next time your pal asks you to go to the club with them, you know why.

However, we tend only to focus on one end of the

spectrum: the rich, beautiful, famous, or successful and pay less attention to the other end. We are made to feel poorer or less successful than we actually are. It's like we are on a treadmill, constantly striving to be happy but getting no closer to achieving this goal. If our standard of living improves and everyone else's remains the same, we feel happier, but if theirs improves too, we don't always feel happier.

Lastly is the intertemporal gap, which is how we form expectations based on our past experiences. We are unhappy when our past is better than our present. Take two workers who earn the same average lifetime income. Worker A's income increased over his/her lifetime while worker B's actually decreased. Research shows that you are always happier when you are worker A even though their current average income is the same. So, why is this? This phenomenon is caused by anchoring; when we compare our present selves to our past selves. If you are constantly improving, exceeding expectations, and moving forward, you are generally happy. And the reverse holds. If you are not improving, meeting, or exceeding your expectations and not moving forward, you are unhappy.

Going forward, you must take a more in-depth look at your expectations and how they stack up to reality and, to some extent, how they affect your mood. Here are some tips on where to start. When faced with a new situation, try and think of what will happen? Is this how your expectations should be? Where are they from, and are they realistic? Whenever you get disappointed, try to think back on whether your expectations were realistic?

Reality is nothing like what we imagine or perceive. It is unbound, and we have no control over it. Control creates expectations, and these set us up for disappointment. If we want to find true happiness, we have to let go of the lies our expectations create. Rather than trying to control the reality around us to satisfy our expectations, we must take stock of what we can control: our minds and our own actions. Happiness comes from within us, not from outside. If we are to build a happy life, then we need to work on what we can control; otherwise, whatever happiness we build for ourselves will never meet our expectations and can collapse anytime. When we find that internal happiness, we carry it with us through the good and bad times, and we are unaffected by external factors. Staying the same goes back to control. We, humans, are averse to change. It frightens us, and we want our zones of comfort. We find solace in the familiar, and this prevents us from growing, self-actualizing.

5

A GOOD LIFE IS BUILT ON GOOD RELATIONSHIPS

"Treasure your relationships, not your possessions."

— ANTHONY J. D'ANGELO

While we must find happiness within ourselves, this doesn't mean ignoring the people around us. We often have very negative, unintentional relationships with those around us, even when they can seem quite positive in the beginning. When we get into relationships, we get trapped into trying to take on a lot of the other people's problems and trying to get them to fix our problems in turn, that we create a psychological image of who we think they are and, in turn, who they think we are. However, this psychological image or the expectations we set are quite far from reality, which only complicates our interpersonal relationships.

It may seem odd to look at relationships after having spoken so much about ourselves and how we are solely responsible for our happiness. However, a large body of research and psychological study highlights the importance of good, healthy relationships (Waldinger, n.d.). They help us to learn, grow, laugh, and love. People with strong broad-ranging social relationships are happier, healthier, and live longer. Good relationships with family and friends provide love, meaning, support, and increase our sense of self-worth. Widening our social networks brings a sense of belonging, so taking action to strengthen our relationships and build quality connections is integral in finding true happiness.

Relationships are the backbone of a meaningful life. When surrounded by others, we tend to define ourselves by our relationships. Humans are not solitary creatures; from birth, we depend on others for survival, both physically and spiritually. Life is just better when we share our wins and losses with others. The quality of the relationships we have largely determine the quality of life we have. If you have loving, supporting relationships, you are generally happier and more open to others. You are easy-going and can take on challenges because you know someone has your back. Your quality of life is good.

The reverse also holds. Devoid of love and support, we feel something is lacking in our lives. Even though happiness comes from within, it is generated by the interactions between our thoughts and the state of our bodies. However, external factors, such as lack of love, support, and loneliness, can heavily influence our internal state. It stands to reason our external environment affects our internal landscape. If you are struggling to find happiness within, changing your external landscape by building good relationships can declutter your internal environment. By purging the things that don't do us any good or bring us joy, we are left with what does. Building good relationships allows us to bring those positive things into view and serves as an example of how to declutter and change our internal state.

Why relationships matter

Relationships contribute to overall happiness and well-being. It's about social connectedness and having love and intimacy in your life through friends, family, and romantic partners. Well-being and happiness drawn from good relationships are characterized by the fact that by caring for others and in turn being cared for, both needs are satisfied. When both put the other's well being ahead of themselves then both are happy. When it comes to social connections, most of us are winging it. We are often swept up and exhilarated by the early stages of love, but the grind of daily life and our personal baggage start to creep in after a while. We find ourselves struggling in the face of hurt, emotional withdrawal, worsening conflict, boredom, and inadequate coping mechanisms. We soon realize that building happy and healthy relationships is hard. It takes work.

There's a lot of research on relationships with scientists trying to figure out what the healthiest and happiest couples are doing right (Waldinger, n.d.). Harvard currently has the longest ongoing study of relationships in human history. The study aims to answer: what makes life good? In the 1930s, Harvard researchers invited several sophomores from the school and teenagers from some of Boston's poorest neighborhoods to participate. They were 19 at the time, and over the next 75 years, they were interviewed, had medical tests done, and checked up on every two years to see how they were doing. What the researchers found out about happiness surprised them.

Many millennials think that fame, fortune, and hard work will bring them happiness; however, they don't. It's the social connections we have that are most vital to our happiness and well-being. But how can someone who worked so hard to earn fame and fortune be unhappy? The Harvard researchers learned the following key lessons. First, good relationships are good for our bodily health and well-being, and that loneliness or being separated from others literally can kill. Secondly, it's the quality, not the quantity of relations that matter. Lastly, good relationships are not only good for your body but also your mind.

What we learn from the longest study on happiness

Sting was at the height of his music career in 1983. The Police, his band, had topped the charts with their recent album, and their song was the most played song on the radio. Albums were flying off shelves; concerts were selling out. It seemed like all was going according to plan. Sting and The Police had a successful music career, all the fame and money they could want, but why did they break up the following year?

The answer is quite simple; pop culture has the wrong idea of happiness because there's a disconnect between what we think, imagine or believe will make us happy versus what actually does. That's why millennials think that all fame and fortune are the keys to happiness. Because pop culture had drummed it into their minds through images and videos, what a life of fame and fortune is like. However, this has nothing to do with finding happiness. The world is littered with unhappy rich people, tormented celebrities, and lonely workaholics.

What makes us truly happy are the good relationships we have. The Harvard researchers found that making social connections is good for your physical health. Those connected to family, friends, and community were happier, physically healthier, and lived longer. And, as I said, it turns out loneliness can kill. The study proved it. Those who were segregated from others or had fewer social connections were often lonely. Loneliness increases the chances of getting a heart attack by over 40 percent and premature death by over 50 percent.

They also determined that it's not the number of connections or relationships you have but the quality that matters. Those who valued quantity over quality had poorer physical health and were less happy than those who had fewer more quality relationships. Focusing on quantity reduces the quality of the connections you make while rescuing the number of relationships you have allows you to focus on and boost their quality. High-quality relationships are resonant, while low-quality ones are dissonant. This means that high-quality relationships are characterized by mutual trust and respect, while low-quality ones are more conflict-prone. The distinction between the two is due to the different neurological networks that form and trigger when we connect with others. Resonant relationships trigger connections in parts of the brain associated with positive emotion. In contrast, dissonant relationships trigger parts of the brain linked to avoidance, decreased compassion and affection, and other negative emotions.

Our brains remember and react to the quality of the connections we make, and it has long influenced various aspects of our physical and psychological health. Ask yourself, are your personal relationships bringing out the best in you? Do they make you a better person? Do you find yourself uplifted whenever you are around your family or friends?

Having high-quality relationships also benefits the mind. The study showed that those with better social relationships had sharper memory, while those in poorer relationships showed a sharp decline in memory. These relationships reduce the risk of getting dementia and other mental decline conditions. Forming quality social connections has been proven to lower anxiety and depression, boost self-esteem, empathy, trust, and cooperation. They also reduce stress, which boosts your immune system too.

The great thing about building good relationships is that they make you happier and more satisfied with life. They protect you from life's stresses and also trigger a flow-on effect where those surrounding you will be drawn into spending more time with you because you are literally a ray of sunshine. In this way, social connectedness creates a positive feedback loop of social, physical, and emotional well-being. People will naturally be attracted to knowing you and being with you.

How mindsets affect relationships

People with a fixed mindset feel threatened and are often hostile when talking about minor issues in how they and their significant other see their relationship. They believe that they are one with their partner and share the same views, so even a minor disagreement can threaten this belief. The most destructive of all relationship myths that those with a fixed mindset have is the belief that if something requires work, then something is terribly wrong and that any difference in opinions or preferences is indicative of a character flaw in their partners. However, by now, you know better. There are no great achievements without setbacks, so there are no great relationships without conflicts and problems along the way.

If you have a fixed mindset whenever you talk about the conflicts in your relationship, you tend to assign blame. Sometimes you blame yourself, but a lot of the time, it's always your partner's fault. This blame is assigned to a trait or a character flaw. As if that's not enough, this blame game causes you to feel anger and disgust toward your partner. And it gets worse: since the issue stems from fixed traits to you, it can't be solved. Once you see flaws in your partner, you become scornful and condescending to them and dissatisfied with the whole relationship.

However, with a growth mindset, you can acknowledge your partner's imperfections, without assigning blame, and still feel that you have a fulfilling relationship. You view conflicts as indicators of communication issues, not as a sign of issues with your personality or character. This dynamic holds true both in romantic partnerships, friendships, and even in your relationship with your parents.

When we set out to build a relationship, we meet someone totally different from us, and we haven't learned how to deal with these differences yet. In a good relationship, we develop these skills by spending time together, showing interest in each other, and emotionally nurturing one another. This grows and deepens the relationship. But for this to occur, we've got to be on the same page or at least feel like we are. As trust develops, we become interested in each other's development. When we form bonds, we tend to adapt to them, often getting complacent in the long run. We take how things are a reality rather than working on them to make our relationships work. Understand you cannot have a perfect relationship; aim for a 5:1 ratio of positive to negative feelings; after all, it's the negative emotions that provide hidden opportunities to learn more about each other.

What all your interactions boil down to is your

mindset. This interpretative process that tells you what's going on around you. The fixed mindset is marred by an internal monologue of constant judging and evaluation, using every piece of information you observe as evidence either for or against assessments such as whether you or someone else is a good person, does he or she have the traits to be a good match for you, or are you better than the person next to you? The internal monologue of the growth mindset, on the flip side, is not as judgmental, but it is eager to learn and hungry for information, constantly on the lookout for the kind of input you can absorb into learning and constructive action.

Building healthy relationships

Many of our relationships are formed accidentally. You probably found your friends or spouse at work, school, the club, or while randomly walking down the street. It happens. It's safe to say that the relationships you have in your life right now are based on proximity. This is because it is simple and convenient for us to form relationships with those we are around most of the time. There's nothing fundamentally wrong with it, except we are not intentional about it. We leave this important decision up to an arbitrary choice such as where we live, work, school, gym, etc.

These relationships are formed because they are

easy and comfortable; however, they may not always be in our best interest. "Show me your mates, and I will tell you the type of person you are." That saying sums it up quite nicely. Given that we are not intentional about the relationships we form, you can see how we leave ourselves open to opportunistic and toxic relationships and social connections.

Look at the relationships in your life right now and ask yourself:

- Does it make me happy?
- Does it give me more than it takes? Conversely, do I give more into it than what I take?
- Does it serve me and the other person or bring us both joy?

I figure there are a few people and relationships who are solid NOs to these questions. Why are you still hanging on? If a relationship no longer makes sense, keeping it won't change that; dropping it may even make you happier. Decluttering your closet and donating some of your old clothes can make you happy; you will feel that you have done some good. The same goes for relationships. Dropping those relationships that no longer make us happy is like decluttering your life. Many of the relationships we have, we keep them because they are convenient, and we want to avoid the emotional effort required to let go. Remember, we are averse to loss, so our minds would rather stay with this than deal with the emotional fallout that marks the end of a relationship.

Just like that pair of jeans that don't fit anymore, these relationships served a purpose, but now they have run their course. They probably made us happy once, so we keep them because of what they represent and because we are too lazy or nostalgic to purge them even though deep down, we know that they will no longer bring us happiness. To be truly happy, we have to let go of the emotional baggage, unhealthy attachments, and relationships that take more than they give. It's the essence of living a happier life. Removing the negative is just as important as adding the positive, and nowhere does it have a bigger impact than on our relationships.

It might seem harsh taking on your relationships with such ruthless precision; however, it's for the best. The only relationships worth building are where both parties benefit from it.

There are three types of social connections you can have:

- **Intimate** – such as those between you and the people you love and care for: your family, friends, and lovers.
- **Relational** – these are formed with the

people you see often and have a shared interest, such as your workmates or business relations.
- **Collective** – these connections are formed between people who share a group membership or affiliation such as the people you go to church with or to the gym with or even people who share your political views.

When building relationships, ask yourself, do you have good, meaningful, long-term relationships in these areas? Maybe you tend to stick with old friends and feel you can't meet new people? Or maybe you are avoiding people from your past mingling with people who know as little about you as possible? Be honest about your relationships and social connections. Think about the relationships you have had and the type of relationships you would like to have. You may find that you would want to try making new friends despite sticking with old ones for so long, or you may want to strengthen existing relationships.

A simple way to bolster existing social connections is to reach out to people you already know, such as family, friends, neighbors, or coworkers, with whom you want to build a good relationship. Give them a call. Write or message them on social media; let them know you'd like to keep in touch more. Plan coffee dates, picnics, go swimming, or play a round of golf together. Think about common interests you share and use that to find things to do together.

To meet new people, you can strike up a conversation with someone you regularly see on the train, bus, gym, or even at your favorite coffee place. You can join a team or volunteer. Engaging in community service is a great way to build social connections. Find out about local groups or programs by visiting your local community center or public library; there's always something happening in your community. Having these fun times will help you develop more positive feelings towards them and share in the happiness that comes from engaging positively with others. The idea behind building good relationships is sharing your time and experiences with the people you want and also listening to them. Remember to be intentional about the relationships and social connections you create. Over time, you will create meaningful and intentional relationships with those you care about that will benefit your mind and body.

That being said, it doesn't mean that you should accept everyone. Remember, I told you to be intentional; relationships are messy, and not every Tom, Dick, and Harry can be your friend. While you may genuinely want to build a good relationship with them, some people are just poisonous. Sometimes it's best to end a toxic relationship no matter what stage it is in.

This intentionality helps ground us in reality rather than floating away into the clouds of expectation as we so often do, especially when relationships come into play. With a clearer view, we can see people for who they are, not who we expect them to be, and we can connect with them better. This allows you to water and nurture the relationships you want, much like flowers in a garden, so that they grow strong and supportive.

6

STRESS

"When I look back on all these worries, I remember the story of an old man who said on his deathbed that he had a lot of trouble in his life, most of which never happened."

— Winston Churchill

Whenever I hear somebody say, "Life's hard," I am tempted to ask, as compared to what?

Life is challenging. Stress is everywhere, and there's no way to avoid it. Chances are, you've probably been in a couple of stressful situations. Getting stuck in traffic, being late for work, missing a deadline, relationship problems, trauma, you name it. While we all undergo varying degrees of stress, there are common elements that must take place every time we are stressed. Ever noticed how your breathing becomes faster, your muscles tense, and your pulse goes up whenever you are stressed out?

We all think we know about stress. How could we not? There are tons of articles, journals, and books talking about stress everywhere. It's even all over the news. However, despite having all this information at our disposal, the general outlook on stress is pretty narrow. What I mean is we are still very close-minded when it comes to stress. I bet you had no idea there is both good and bad stress. Yes, you read that right. There's good stress. But I'm getting ahead of myself here. We need to go through some of the basics first.

What is stress?

What was the first thing you thought about when you saw this chapter about stress? Is it your overbearing boss or partner? Maybe it's your laughable financial situation? Perhaps it could even be that your marriage or relationship is ending? Whatever you thought about just now, that feeling it elicits in you, that's stress. We are all familiar with it and experience it from time to time, but if someone asked you to define stress, perhaps you'd be at a loss for words.

Come to think of it, many of us only realize we are stressed when we are on the edge about to break.

Defining stress is as hard as defining happiness because of its subjective nature. However, there exists a scientific definition nonetheless. Stress can be defined as your body's nonspecific reaction to the demands imposed by change. It's how your body reacts to a challenge or demand. Think of it as a feeling of emotional or physical tension throughout your body. The term was coined by Hans Selye, a Hungarian-Canadian endocrinologist who researched stress and how it affected the body (Tan, S. Y., & Yip, A, 2018).

He claimed that stress be it good or bad, was stressful, meaning it causes the same body reaction. His research into stress began after observing how patients with different chronic diseases had the same symptoms. He named this set of similar responses the General Adaptation Syndrome. This syndrome takes place in three phases: the alarm, adaptation, and exhaustion phase. These phases describe the things that go on in our bodies whenever we are stressed.

The alarm phase refers to the initial stages of stress, when the flight or fight response kicks in, more aptly named the stress response, is triggered. Remember feeling your pulse and breathing quicken? It all happens here. At this stage, your body releases cortisol, or the stress hormone, to increase your energy and alert your muscles in anticipation of what might happen. The adaptation stage quickly follows, and your body begins reverting back to the state it was before the stress response kicked in. Cortisol levels are reduced, and your heart rate and breathing regulate. You basically go back to normal.

If the cause of your stress is resolved, your body continues healing, but if that's not the case, your body remains in alarm mode. If your stress persists, your body will remain in this heightened state of alertness and eventually adapt to it. Your body will then change as it continues secreting cortisol and other hormones to keep you alert. This means your pulse, breathing, and blood pressure will remain high. You may also exhibit irritability, frustration, and problems concentrating. If the adaptation stage continues for too long without pause or ending, it turns into chronic stress, and that right there will kill you.

There are two types of stress: acute and chronic. Acute stress is temporary stress, the type that comes and goes quickly. We all experience instances of acute stress, such as when we are running late for work. A single instance of acute stress is not harmful, far from it. It actually offers more pros than cons. However, it still causes physical symptoms such as headaches, high blood pressure, or mild stomach problems. Repeated instances of acute stress can lead to disorders such as acute stress disorder and chronic stress.

Chronic stress can be defined as stress experienced

over long periods. When you stress over your finances, relationships, careers, family, etc., we are under chronic stress because we think about these things every day without end. This right here is the real bad guy. It's regarded as the most harmful type of stress as it can eat away at us emotionally, physically, and mentally. The thing is, we never realize we are suffering from chronic stress until it's too late. It's the adverse physical symptoms such as burnout that tell us that something is wrong.

With chronic stress, we become used to living in a heightened state of awareness and the emotions generated in this state. Unlike acute stress, there's no coming down from this ride. Acute stress is short-lived because we find immediate solutions; however, finding the solutions to our chronic stressors is harder. Therefore, chronic stress becomes a part of you and your personality because you are unable to deal with it. This makes you prone to even more stress and its adverse effects. Decoded, you become a walking zombie, dead man walking here.

Let me explain why.

You see, stress, whether it's short or long term, causes health issues. Remember the changes our bodies go through whenever we are stressed? Let's go over that again. When the stress response is activated, your body discharges adrenaline, cortisol, and other hormones, which causes your heart rate and breathing to quicken. Your muscles get tense in anticipation of what will happen. It's fight or flight. Any bodily system that can't help you get out of this perceived danger you are in, such as your digestive system is slowed down. That's why it's hard to eat sometimes when you're stressed. Because the heart is pumping so hard, you get tension headaches but these eventually blow over.

Now, imagine if you lived in this state every minute of every day? With your heart beating like crazy, you'd get heart problems and high blood pressure. Gastrointestinal issues come next, the ulcers, heartburn, gas, indigestion, and then the mental stuff, migraines, anxiety, panic attacks, depression, and even memory loss because your whole body is out of sorts. Before you know it, now you're on five different types of medication, all trying to keep you alive. Case in point: you are now a zombie, like the other three billion zombies in the world.

What you need to understand is, long term stress can cause irreparable damage to our bodies. Why wait until you have heart problems to start dealing with your stress?

Despite all this, many of us are unaware of how badly stress is affecting us. The stress response is triggered automatically and too often, denying your body the time it needs to recover. Many times we feel like we have no control over it. That it's an outside force that is wreaking havoc in our lives freely, but that isn't true.

There are various techniques and tips you can utilize to manage and control stress, even get it to work for us.

The right kind of stress

Stress is the bad guy, that much is clear. But what if it could make you better...even happier? We have been known to make the best of bad situations, so why not with stress? When life gives you lemons, make lemonade. In a lot of happiness approaches, stress reduction and management is a recurrent theme. It's hard to be satisfied with life when you are anxious. Yet oddly enough, researchers have found that consciously putting stress and pressure on yourself can indeed make you better and happier.

Research distributed in the *Journal of Happiness Studies* (yes, it exists) stated that those who work hard at improving a skill or ability experience stress, but they also experience greater fulfillment and satisfaction with their daily progress in the long run. Working to learn a new skill or accomplish a goal means more stress now, but it also means happiness later. By engaging in behaviors aimed at increasing our competence, say at work, school, gym, and so on, we experience a momentary decrease in happiness and enjoyment and an increase in stress. However, despite the negatives we experience in the present, these same activities make us feel happy and satisfied when we look back at them as a whole. Doing those crunches sucked, but at the end of the day, you are happy with your abs.

This finding suggests that to become proficient at something, we need to endure momentary stress to reap the happiness benefits linked with increasing competency. No pain, no gain. That's the only rule when it comes to getting happiness from gaining an ability. This is why oftentimes we give up on our goals because they are too stressful, but at the end of the day, there's a benefit at learning to do something. What's even more surprising is we don't have to reach our goals to become happier and improve our well-being. The act of doing is the benefit by itself. If you can power through the added short term stress, you stand to make huge gains in well-being and happiness long-term.

Trying new things is stressful, so is learning anything; working towards a huge goal such as living a happier life is also stressful, downright hard. However, focusing on the goal and accomplishing it makes you feel good. You accomplished what you wanted but even just the act of trying and giving it your best makes you feel good. It's all about the journey, not necessarily the destination. This feeling has a domino effect as it gives you the motivation you need to do what you have to do today, tomorrow, and the day after that. It's the small successes that motivate us the most. Savoring these wins makes you feel good about yourself, and you should not feel the need to compare yourself to others. If you can feel better about yourself today, you get to get this feeling for years to come...and nobody can take that away from you.

All of this won't be possible if you can't control your stress levels. I mean, we are talking about consciously putting yourself in a stressful situation. If you can't handle the stress you have now, this won't work. Rather than serve as a motivator, the added stress will have fun wrecking your life.

Identifying stressors

To deal with stress effectively, you have to know what's stressing you. This way, you can come up with strategies to deal with them. Knowing what's causing stress in your life is the first step to dealing with it. Stress-inducing factors or stressors are any elements that trigger your stress response. Figuring out what your stressors are seems pretty straight forward, but sometimes getting to the root cause of your stress can be harder than it sounds. This is mostly because we are so good at projecting. Rather than deal with an issue as it is, we project it onto someone or something else. They become the bad guy when, in reality, they aren't.

With acute stress, it's easy to identify what's stressing you, however with chronic stress, it's buried under so many other things that it can be hard to pinpoint exactly what's bugging you. As if that's not enough, we don't realize we have chronic stress until it's too late meaning we are already suffering from whatever triggered the stress response and all the other stuff on top of it – burying it. Sure sometimes we are aware of what's stressing us, say a deadline, but maybe it's not the demands of the job or the deadline but the procrastination habit that's really stressing you. Stressors can be anything, from our thoughts, feelings, attitude, emotions, habits, etc. They all contribute to our overall stress levels in a way.

To identify your stressors, you have to dig deep, examine everything from your thoughts, habits, behaviors, attitudes, aptitudes, the whole shebang.

- Do you find yourself justifying away stress as short-term, even though you can't remember the last time you relaxed? "I have so much to do right now. I'll relax once I'm done."
- Do you label stress as a fundamental part of your home or work life? "Work is always hectic." "I have three kids; I'm lucky if I get any sleep." Or do you use it to define your personality? "I'm highly strung. That's all."
- Do you often blame your stress on circumstances or others? "My supervisor is

overworking me." Or do you view the situation as a normal occurrence? "It's nothing new – being a parent is quite demanding, but I am used to it."

Any of this sound familiar?

Until you accept the part you play in creating and maintaining your overall stress, it will always be out of your control. Yes. *You stress yourself out too.*

Stressors can be split into two groups: external and internal stressors. External stressors include things that happen to you, such as traumatic events, workplace stress, and other environmental factors. Internal stressors, as the name suggests, are pretty much self-induced. They include all the thoughts, feelings, and emotions you lug around that cause you to worry. Examples include your anxiety, apparent lack of control and let's not forget your fears.

Emotional stress, a type of chronic stress triggered by your emotions, in case you didn't get that, can hit harder than other types of stress. For instance, when you fight with a loved one. The stress-induced in such a case tends to cause a greater physical reaction and a more profound sense of distress than an episode of acute stress. Emotional stress often leads to anxiety, anger, rumination, and other strong emotional reactions that can take quite a toll on your body. It's easy to project our emotional stressors onto other factors and thus make identifying and dealing with them even harder. How do you identify them?

Emotional stressors can include your fears and anxiety over unknown situations, worrying what others will think of you, say at your new job, or a date. Certain personality traits such as perfectionism, pessimism, hopelessness, or paranoia can also cause emotional stress. These stressors shape how you think, how you perceive yourself, and even your view of others. They are so individualistic that how they affect you isn't how they'll affect someone else.

OTHER STRESSORS INCLUDE:

1. **Family** – for instance, changes in your family life such as death, the birth of a baby, getting married, relationship status, empty-nest syndrome, financial problems, moving residences, etc.
2. **Social** – these come whenever you interact with others, such as going on a date, attending a party, or even addressing people publicly. Similar to emotional stressors, they are also individualized; your friend may love public speaking but the thought of standing in front of an audience might not be for you.

3. **Change** – these come about when you are dealing with a major change in your life, whether positive or negative. It can be getting hitched, buying a house, a break-up, divorce, death in the family, or losing your job.
4. **Work** – these are related to the demands of your job. They can include tight deadlines, an unpredictable and overbearing boss, etc.
5. **Chemical** – these include any drugs you are abusing in a misguided effort to curb your chronic stress. This includes alcohol, nicotine, caffeine, or even pills. A lot of the time, they only worsen the situation. As if that wasn't obvious already.
6. **Physical** – they can include things that overwork or tax your body, such as not getting enough sleep, not eating well, being uncomfortable, pregnancy, exercise, etc.
7. **Making decisions**– decision stressors include any decision-making instance that might induce stress such as picking when to get a baby, selecting a career, etc.
8. **Phobias** – these include any situation that you might find yourself in that triggers your phobias, such as flying, bungee jumping, getting dirty, being in confined spaces, etc.

This isn't even an exhaustive list. Stressors can be anything, as long as they induce a stress reaction from you. This list is meant to give you a rough idea of some of the things that might be low-key stressing you. You'll find that your stressors fall into multiple categories.

Examine this list and see which of your stressors are within your control and influence circle. If cleaning your apartment on your day off is eating into your time off, consider getting a cleaning service to do it. If pressing your clothes is causing you to go to bed too late, consider sending them to the cleaners or buying wrinkle-free clothes. If this is a bit pricey, try and rearrange your monthly budget and allocate some cash for these services, so you can get more time to rest because your time is valuable, too. Isn't that why you are working so hard? So you can live a good life?

You can't entirely eliminate stressors; what you can do is reduce their potency. For example, if work is too noisy, try getting some earplugs. If your commute is two hours long through heavy traffic, consider relocating; if that is not feasible, try carpooling or using public transportation options as you relax listening to some tunes or even take a nap.

Managing stress in pursuit of happiness

"It's not the load that breaks you but how you carry it." – Lou Holtz

This saying exemplifies what stress is all about. It's not about how much stress you are under but how you choose to deal with it. That's what makes or breaks you.

"One is given strength to bear what happens to one, but not the one hundred and one different things that might happen." – C.S. Lewis

With stress, you can only manage the things that have happened to you, what's within your circle of control and influence, not the other billion things that could happen. To effectively learn how to deal with stress, you have to fundamentally change your relationship with it. Understand you are not powerless, and stress can be overcome. Here are a few ways you can do that.

1. **Breathe** – this is one of those quick fixes. Breathing exercises can help bring your pulse and breathing down. Breathe in deeply and fill your belly with air. Slowly count to five, then exhale through your mouth as you count to five again. Imagine inhaling peaceful, calming air and spreading it all over your body. As you exhale, you let go of the tensions and stress... washed away by the peaceful air you took in.
2. **Progressive muscle relaxation (PMR)** – this

muscle relaxation technique helps reduce body tension and stress. It involves contracting and then releasing different muscles in your body and thus releasing the tension they held. For instance, you can clench your fist count to ten as you breathe deeply and then release. It's proven to reduce your stress reactivity and susceptibility to chronic stress.

3. **Journal** – whenever you feel yourself getting stressed, take out your journal and write about it. What happened? What caused the stress? How did you feel? How did you handle it? Rant in there. Are you feeling better now? Spare no detail. Get it all out. This will serve as a log to help you identify any recurrent themes that might be causing your stress. Writing down how you feel can offer relief, reduce stress, and even keep other mental problems at bay. However, you have to journal consistently. It might not be every day; even weekly will do; just don't stop journaling.

4. **Exercise and eat right**– you aren't going to get away from this one. There are numerous perks of working out and maintaining a healthy diet, including releasing feel-good hormones such as dopamine that help fight

the effects of stress. Eat food that fuels your body and boosts your mood too. You don't have to take on grueling exercises, why not try yoga, tai chi, aerobics, Zumba, etc.

5. **Practice mindfulness and meditate** – meditation and mindfulness are great techniques for dealing with short and long-term stress. There are so many ways you can meditate and be mindful that there's something to fit everyone. Mindful meditation involves taking in the moment, identifying your thoughts, and not being judgmental about them while being aware of what's around you, the tastes, smells, sounds, etc. When you are focused on the now, you can't keep thinking or worrying about what happened or might happen. While mindfulness and meditation are powerful skills to have in the fight against stress, they take quite a bit of practice to master. But this is nothing compared to the difference they make in your overall stress levels.

6. **Have supportive relationships** – told you good relationships reduce stress and make you happier. They offer a stress-coping mechanism, so if you feel overwhelmed, talking to a trusted friend or partner can

help you deal with it. They offer emotional support displayed through the tight hugs, listening, and empathizing ears loved ones offer. You also get informational support that can help you deal with particularly stressful and tricky situations.

7. **Manage your expectations** – remember the expectation gap we talked about earlier? When reality falls short, it can be disappointing and stressful. We imagined something being better than it actually is, and when it turns out bad, we get stressed, worrying why this is so. Don't you think this is stupid? If you focus on how things are, you won't get as disappointed. You see the positive more easily, and you're less strung out. This allows you to appreciate and be grateful for what you have rather than pining over what you expect to have. Quick exercise: what are you grateful for today?

8. **Remove the load** – get a hug, take a walk, listen to music, eliminate stressors, cut down on caffeine, laugh, dance, take time off: basically, take a load off. That's how you can deal with stress.

We are all neck-deep in stress that we don't even question it. We just roll over and accept it. This shouldn't be the case. We shouldn't be carrying stress with us like its normal. These stress management techniques are meant to act as quick fixes and help you in the long term by increasing your resilience to stressors. Find a combination of techniques to identify, diffuse, and overcome your stress. Stress used and managed properly can contribute to improving your life and achieving happiness.

7

FAIL MORE

*"To try and fail is at least to learn;
to fail to try is to suffer the inestimable loss
of what might have been."*

— Chester Barnard

Contrary to popular belief, failure is not the opposite of success. Far too long, we've been fed this narrative that failure cannot coexist with success, that it is the enemy, something that should be avoided at all costs. And so we have strived to avoid failure in everything we do. But everyone fails. It's inevitable; in fact, we probably fail at something every day. But does it mean we are failures?

A lot of successful people failed countless times before they became a success. There's no success story that wasn't founded in failure. How many times did Babe Ruth strike-out before he made record home runs? How many recipes of KFC's failed before they got the right one? How many shots did Jordan miss before he became the GOAT (the greatest of all time)? 9,000. That's how many. He lost over three hundred games in his career; 26 times, he was trusted to take the game-winning shot for his team and missed. But he is regarded as the greatest basketball player of all time.

A notable persona in online publications, Arianna Huffington, was rejected by 36 publishers before publication. Even *The Huffington Post* was not a success right away. It got a lot of bad reviews, with many doubting its potential. Obviously, Arianna didn't let her failure hold her back and turned *The Huffington Post* into an empire. Before Bill Gates created Microsoft, he entered the entrepreneurial scene with a company called Traf-O-Data, which was aimed at processing and analyzing data from traffic tapes. Think of it as a precursor to Big Data. Even then, he was a genius; however, this venture tanked. He was unable to sell it because the product barely worked. But he regrouped and brought us Microsoft, forging a new path to success.

Walt Disney, the guy behind so many lovable characters such as Mickey and Minnie, was told he had no creativity. His first company Laugh-O-Gram failed after a partner pulled out. Desperate and out of money, he faced a lot of ridicule, failure, and more criticism before his first few films became famous, and the Disney you know today was born. When you form a company, job security isn't something you worry about. In his 20s, Steve Jobs found success when Apple became a huge hit. However, in his 30s, the company's board of directors fired him. Unfazed by failure, he founded a new company, NeXT, that was eventually acquired by Apple. Once back there, he proved his capacity for success by reinventing Apple leading it to new heights.

Jordan, Babe Ruth, Colonel Sanders, Bill Gates, Steve Jobs, and a lot of other successful people have failed massively, sometimes so badly that it looked like the end. Do you think they let these failures or setbacks get them down?

Whenever we fail, our expectations are dashed. In the moment, failure seems like the end, but it's not. How you perceive it is what matters. Admitting that failure is part of the learning process can help reduce the fear and anxiety around it. It can also reduce the negative self-reflection that we are bad because we failed. Failing means we get to learn something. It means we tried to do something new, embraced change, and helps prepare us for success.

Why failure has a bad reputation

While I'm all for trying and failing, understand

that there are real consequences to failing. Not succeeding can be disappointing and painful. To make it worse, we as a society have glorified winning and demonized failing, such that we only celebrate our successes and not the struggles we go through to get there. Winning isn't everything; it becomes the only thing. With this all or nothing mindset, we take on life with a closed view. We either win or lose, and losers are never remembered. But life is not like that, it's full of ups and downs, and you can't be up every time.

Other than the disappointment and pain we feel when we fail, there are other hidden consequences that run deeper and are more damaging and crippling. These consequences matter because they impact our future efforts and how we feel about ourselves. Whenever we face failure, two things happen:

- We shut down because the shame of falling weighs on us like an anvil and feels like a hammer to the head. We close ourselves off to challenges and new ideas. We basically stop learning.
- We view failure as something that must be avoided at all costs. But this is impossible given that failure is a part of the learning process. This misconstrued view of failure causes us to stop trying because if we don't try, we can't fail.

When this happens, we internalize the fear of failure, which spawns a vicious cycle of procrastination and avoidance. Let's imagine this hypothetical. Dan was terrified that he wouldn't get a job after college. His fear of failing to get the right job made him delay applying for jobs, and so he missed out on some great opportunities. His peers, on the other hand, applied and got these jobs. Now he felt ashamed that he failed to start working on time just as his peers had. This led to further procrastination. There was a career center at the college where Dan went; however, he never used it. His fear kept him trapped and unable to use all the resources available.

Sound familiar?

That's what fearing failure does. It traps you in this cocoon where you are absorbed in all these negative emotions such as shame and disappointment that you close your mind off to everything available to you. Had Dan gone to the career center, he would have gotten the help he needed and probably landed a job. When we choose to try something new, our fear of getting it wrong can be crippling. It hinders our ability to learn, be present, and give it our best shot. Instead, we are preoccupied with what-ifs. What if we fail, what then? These what-ifs convince us to wait for the perfect conditions, which unfortunately don't exist. We create a self-fulfilling prophecy where our fear of failing leads us to putting off practicing, participating, or getting help, thus increasing our chances of failing. It's like we want to fail. We then generalize ourselves as failures and spiral into hopelessness and even depression.

BENEFITS OF FAILURE

The Oxford dictionary defines failure as "not successful. then, it's divided into 'countable' and 'uncountable'. [uncountable] lack of success in doing or achieving something. [countable] a person or thing that is not successful." Simple enough, right? However, somewhere along the line, we misconstrued this simple definition and derived our own translation. We define failure as being a let-down, unworthy, and useless. How did we get all that from the previous definition? This definition alone shows that failure isn't as bad as we think. In fact, it is actually good for us. Interesting isn't it? Thinking of failure as a good thing. As we move on, I want you to think of failure as "doing things the way we anticipated or hoped they would turn out to be although the result might be different is a good thing."

HERE ARE A FEW BENEFITS OF FAILURE:

- It provides a reality check

Nothing transports us back to reality faster than failure. When you fail, you are devastated. But failing allows you to look back at the whole situation in a new light. Ever since Sarah was 12, she always dreamed of going to college. If she made it, she'd be the first member of her family to ever go to college. This was huge for her and her family. She knew that if she didn't get good grades, she'd lose her chance. On top of that, her career advisor would tell her that she wasn't academic enough to get into college. What? She took AP classes. However, Sarah failed, despite wanting this more than anything. But why? Simply put, she wasn't in the right frame of mind. The added pressure from the extra classes, the impression she is not academic enough, and her whole family's hopes and dreams made her think that failure was not an option. All this had a bad effect on her studying and eventually caused her to fail. Sometimes failing at something, even if you truly desire it, serves as an indicator that something isn't right somewhere. Failure helps reveal what's really going on in your situation.

- It's a learning experience

Failure is a great, somewhat harsh teacher. In your life, career, finances, and life goals learning what not to do is just as crucial as learning what to do. You can't have one without the other. Failure leaves you room to right yourself and allows you to learn from your mistakes. This helps you recommit to your goals because now you know what to do and the countless other tries of what not to do.

- It builds character

When you fail, you gain insight into yourself and the task at hand. Anyone can be a hero in good times, but how do you measure up when the going gets tough? Does the pressure get to you, and you crumble, or do you stand your ground and keep fighting? While failure can shake us to our core, going through it tests your character, courage, determination, and mindset. Without it, you can't truly appreciate your best until you have been through failure. It serves a benchmark to show you what you are made of – hopefully, steel.

- It builds creativity and innovation

Failure opens you up to more probabilities and approaches. You are not afraid to think outside the box because failure pushes you to re-evaluate your goals and efforts. When we fail, we get the chance to try again and implement what we learned from our failed attempts. We don't live in a one-shot only world and the problems we face often require creative solutions. There's no clear cut path to happiness; we have to adapt it to our unique situations. Fail, fail, and fail again. That way, you figure out what makes you happy, what doesn't, and creative solutions to getting things done and getting there.

- It fosters resilience

Failure can deal some pretty painful blows. However, it's impossible to live without failure. Doing so will make you cautious of everything. What kind of life is that? And won't you, in essence, have failed at living? You won't learn how to ride a bicycle without falling off a couple of times. You'll probably get a lot of scratches and scrapes, but after failing over and over again, you'll get the hang of it. Failing helps develop resilience. Learning from your failures helps you recover quicker. After falling off the bike, you know what to do to stay on. It makes you stronger so you can easily face any new challenges. Keep moving forward, keep fighting despite the setbacks you face.

- Fearing failure is worse than failure itself

Fear, fear, fear. It seems like everything that keeps us from achieving our goals is fear-related, fear of change, fear of failure, and so on. There's no real alternative to failure; you can choose to try something new and have a 50 percent chance of failing or not try and be sure to fail 100 percent. If you genuinely want to be happier, you have to change some things, and that leaves you open to failure. Even though you don't know how it will turn out, you need to try out new things and take risks. When you fail, you will get a chance to learn from your failure meaning you can take intelligent risks next time and increase your chances of success. The fear of failure stops you from trying, and that is the biggest failure of all.

Coping with failure

Learning how to cope with failure takes some of the fear out of failing. It makes it easier to embrace it and even reduces the pain you feel so you can bounce back better than before. Failure allows you to appreciate where you are in your journey, even if it's not where you wanted to be. Every failure has its purpose. Learn from it. Here are various ways you can cope with failure and everything it elicits.

1. Don't take it personally

If nothing else sticks, remember this one. *Don't take failure personally.* Everyone fails; it's part of the success process, and there's no way around it. You must learn to separate failure from your personal identity. It is not a trait you have; it's a part of life. Just because the idea you had failed, it doesn't mean you are a failure. Failing comes with a lot of emotions, and if you take them all to heart, bouncing back from it becomes a momentous task. Failure is not about your value as a person. It doesn't change your overall worth to your family, friends, or community. It's simply showing what works and what doesn't so you can change accordingly.

2. Ask why

To move forward from failure, we must know what went wrong in the first place. If not, how are we going to figure out what we need to change? Take for example, a job presentation, when it doesn't go according to plan, take some time, and reflect on it. Did you cover everything you needed to? Did you have the right team backing you up? Did you do enough research? Whatever the reason is, find out what it is so that you can make the necessary changes or else you are doomed to repeat your failure.

3. Deal with your emotions

A lot of emotions accompany failure: anxiety, shame, embarrassment, anger, sadness, etc. These are uncomfortable feelings, and we will do anything to escape from them. Remember, our minds are wired to avoid pain, and if failure causes pain, then our brains will work extra hard to keep us from feeling that discomfort. A study published in the *Journal of Behavioral Decision Making* stated that we shouldn't try to brush off or avoid dealing with the feelings elicited by failure (Nelson, et al., 2017). Dealing with your emotions will help you recognize any unhealthy attempts to reduce pain. Not dealing with the emotions you have causes you to find other ways to distract yourself from the pain and fill the void with food, drugs, love, an unhealthy obsession with money, looks, etc. but they won't heal your pain; they only provide temporary relief.

By mindfully reflecting on these, we can learn a lot about ourselves. Embrace that anger, disappointment, and sadness you feel. When things don't go your way, have a good hysterical moment, feel the emotions; don't try to fight or ignore it. Afterwards, make yourself a drink and take the edge off. You'll be able to see things more clearly now. Allowing yourself to feel bad about your failure can serve as motivation. It can push you to work harder and find better solutions so you will improve next time.

4. Be *brutally honest* and take responsibility

Take a long hard look at yourself. Mostly when we fail, we are quick to try and fix the situation rather than reflect on what happened. Distractions can derail us from self-reflection in the wake of failure; however, this is a significant part of the process. We hate confronting ourselves with our mistakes, yet this is the only way we can learn from them. When we are honest about what happened, we can own up to our mistakes. We are able to find explanations and identify the reasons behind the failure and the part we played rather than coming up with excuses and blaming others.

5. Practice healthy stress coping skills

Call a trusted friend, practice some deep breathing techniques, take a relaxing bubble bath, play some music, or dance. These are a few examples of how you can cope with stress healthily. Like I said in the previous chapter, find what works for you. Failing can be stressful, and if you struggle with bad habits whenever you are stressed, such as drinking or smoking, they can worsen. Create a list of healthy stress coping skills and techniques you can use and place them somewhere you can easily see. Use this list to remind you that there are healthier strategies you can turn to whenever you are feeling bad.

6. Make adjustments – fast

After coming to terms with everything, the fact you failed and why you failed, ask yourself, what can I adjust to make things better? Did you set very high expectations? Or maybe you didn't give it all you could? Whatever it may be, failure is a learning opportunity. Find out what you need to change and make sure you don't make the same mistake again. *Failing isn't bad, but failing the same way over and over again is.*

7. Fail forward

You fail forward by studying your mistakes and setbacks. Look at what you can learn and make the necessary arrangements when creating a plan to move forward. If you are open to learning, failure can be a great teacher. Did you make one mistake or a series of them that ultimately led to your failure? What can you do differently next time? Even as you think of all this, don't keep replaying your failures in your head. If you allow yourself to ruminate on everything that went wrong, you'll get stuck in this black hole of despair and hopelessness. Fail forward; see where you went wrong and factor this in when creating a plan to move forward.

8. Be realistic about your goals and failure

Our expectations can set us up. We must always

create realistic expectations and SMART goals. We are more likely to sabotage ourselves when we are convinced that one mistake makes us a total failure. It can be easy to think that tossing your goals out would solve the problem. However, that would be a horrific misunderstanding of the intentions of this book. I'm not saying don't set any goals, just be SMART about them. They should be Specific, Measurable, Achievable, Realistic, and Time-bound. I want you to focus on the realistic part. Don't go aiming for the moon, then hate yourself for falling short. If you do aim for the moon and hit the stars, know that that was your plan after all. You actually succeeded. Take failure as part of the process, and accept all the irrational beliefs you have about it. These often feed your fear of failure, so to remind yourself to have more realistic thoughts about failure, remember:

- Failure shows you are challenging yourself
- Don't take it personally
- You can handle failing; after all, it's a great opportunity to learn.

Repeat these declarations over and over again to help you remain realistic about failure and bounce back.

We cannot stop obstacles from appearing in our lives, but we can choose how to handle them. In your pursuit of happiness, you are bound to face many failures along the way. Don't be afraid of failing. For instance, changing your habits is not easy; a lot of the parts of this journey are hard, and you will fail. However, this shouldn't stop you from persevering. You might discover new opportunities and even learn to see yourself in a more positive light and not as the loser you always thought you were.

THE NEW NORMAL

"When we are no longer able to change a situation, we are challenged to change ourselves."

— Victor Frankl

Finding happiness is a journey, and nothing has reaffirmed this more than the COVID-19 outbreak and all the different natural phenomena happening in 2020. The recent pandemic and consequent global lockdown have cast a dark shadow across the whole world. Each passing day, the impact of the virus grows. Loved ones are dying; we are losing jobs, businesses are closing; basically, everything seems to be getting worse. This whole situation is taking a toll on our mental health, with studies showing more than 60 percent of people reporting that the coronavirus has negatively affected their mental well-being. Only about 49 percent of people felt that their lives were thriving despite everything, the lowest level of life satisfaction recorded since the 2008 financial crisis.

Quarantine has resulted in a rise in depression cases; humans are social creatures. While experts and governments are giving clear guidelines on how to stay safe, it's a lot harder to look after how you feel. The pandemic has plunged our lives into uncertainty, and this is causing anxiety and fear in a lot of people. Our social media and traditional media feeds are now swamped with daily updates on the coronavirus outbreak. You switch on the TV, and every channel you flip to is showing you the pandemic statistics, including death tolls, infection rates, and how many people have recovered. Everywhere you look, someone or something is urging you to stay vigilant and change your routines to help flatten the curve.

The onslaught of rapidly changing updates all reporting the worst-case scenarios can fuel panic and fear. Consuming this information uncritically is a surefire way of eroding the one thing that can help you weather this storm: your mental health. Even before the pandemic, anxiety, and depression cases were on the rise so much so that they were a defining feature of our times. We are a lot less happy in this day and age, and COVID-19 is only making things worse. The uncertainty and isolation are doing very little to help us deal with our new reality – working, schooling, and even taking care of our family virtually. All this compounded by the stress of dealing with unfamiliar circumstances.

How can you be happy during something as devastating as the coronavirus pandemic?

COVID-19 isn't going away soon; we have to find ways to stay calmer and happier long term. Understanding how the virus and the measure put in place to mitigate its spread affect our mental health can help us adapt. Are you experiencing a heady cocktail of emotions right now? Probably some fear, anxiety, confusion, and a bit of loneliness thrown in there for good measure? How will you handle all that and find fulfillment? How can we boost our mental health in this pandemic era to minimize the impact of social distancing and isolation as well as develop a healthier, more resilient new normal for our mental health and overall happiness for the future?

A big part of finding these answers lies in recognizing the relationship between stress regulation, our overall health, and well-being. Why? Because they are all linked. Sicknesses caused by stress can be improved by having good mental health.

During this crisis, our health, both mental and physical, has come into focus, and we have learned that they are our biggest investments. Investing in our health has long-lasting benefits, including surviving a pandemic.

Pandemic life

The Pandemic has changed life as we know it.

For students, it has been a frustrating and uncertain time. Were you able to walk on stage and graduate? Were you able to celebrate this momentous stage in your life? Did you get into college? How was freshman week? Is it what you pictured? How is your virtual or blended learning coming along? What challenges are you facing incorporating technology in your learning? What concerns do you have attending classes in person?

If you are the educator, how are you re-structuring the classroom? How are you ensuring that all safety protocols are being followed such as using masks and social distancing? How is the students' compliance? How are the parents taking everything? What challenges are virtual or blended learning bringing? How have they changed how you teach? How is your workload? What are the things you have to learn or re-learn to teach in this new paradigm?

As a parent, how did you decide to send your child back to school or not? Which option did you pick: in-person learning or blended? Was deciding this difficult? Should they go back to school and trust that the educators will make all the necessary adjustments or let them stay home so that you can protect the seniors in your home but risk them lagging behind? What about those who chose blended learning? Has it been hard making arrangements for someone to stay with your not-old-enough child at home while you work? Or are you torn between staying at home to take care of the children and your aging parents or going to work?

If you had a job, has the experience been stressful? Are you still working? If so, how's the work commute? Are you taking public transport? Are you observing safety protocols or risking your health just to earn a living? How about the changes needed in your workplace? How is everyone taking it? If you are not working, did you get laid off or can't find work or you simply chose not to work because of the kids and senior relatives at home? How are you paying the bills? Were you able to get deferements? How about those that are past due? Are you able to pay your rent or mortgage? Is it just a deferment or government subsidy able to settle that? Are you still receiving those government subsidy checks? If not, do you have any idea when they will come back? Do you think it will be too late if all the politicians keep bickering about your future instead of just doing it?

If you are the landlord, is it frustrating that the

onus has been put on you? As the government asks you to defer rent, has the bank or private lender you owe mortgage or loans to deferred your payments? Aren't you like most just trying to also make a living? Didn't you risk your own life savings and make sacrifices for that rental property and now you are being asked to make more concessions and sacrifices while some are even vilifying you?

How about the business owners? Have you ever wondered what you did wrong when the government shut down everything and now you are on the brink of closure? What about all the workers and their families you are responsible for? What about your family you are responsible for? All your sacrifices and hard-earned money are gone within the last half of this year. How long can you hold on and keep your doors open? After that, then what?

If you are in the different sectors, whether it be the airlines, tourism and travel, accommodation, transportation, retail, wholesale, industrial, trading, government, financial, food, manufacturing, peacekeeping and all the other sectors, we were and are still all touched and being affected and changed by this pandemic. The normal we know has radically changed. There are many that are looking forward to when we can all go back to the life we knew before all this happened – hopefully, when we all get the vaccines and this is all over. The question is, will we ever go back to those times? When will this be really over? Are the vaccines really the answer? Think of the common flu or colds. Have we really eradicated those with vaccines? We have had the common cold and flu for a very long time and no amount of vaccines have eradicated them. They all come back every year during the flu season and seasons in between. Think about other diseases. We still have no definitive cure for cancer or HIV. We are managing them but they are not totally eradicated. When did we really get a handle on diphtheria? The vaccine was developed in 1921 but even now 5,000 people die from this disease annually (Wagner, 1986). How about Hib Flu? The first vaccine was licensed in 1985 and yet up to now there are 450,000 children dying from its complications annually. How about measles? The first vaccine was developed in 1963 and there has been a 99 percent drop in measles cases but according to WHO there has been still 400,000 to 800,000 deaths annually in 2006. Do you get the point? How about herd immunity? Have we even contemplated how many lives will be lost just to achieve that? Have we considered people who will not even be willing to get vaccinated? On top of that, how long before we can achieve that? I hate to be the party pooper but reality is, this virus will stay with us for a very long time. The changes we are seeing might not be as temporary as we thought they would be. We will contain and manage the virus but do you honestly think we will totally eradicate it in a short period of time?

If that is the case then, what should we do? Should we just panic, treat each other as trash and destroy whatever is left of our environment and the systems we built as a civilization?

Post-pandemic life

Make no mistake about it, this is what the future looks like now. There might be a few changes here and there but this is pretty much it; social distancing, wearing masks everywhere, washing hands, social bubbles, virtual learning, video meetings, elbow bumps instead of handshakes, working from home, mass migration from crowded cities, the boom of online retail, and the decline of the brick and mortar shops.You are also going to see a boom in the shipping industry and freelancing, fewer office and commercial spaces rented due to the closures and outward migration, increase in sanitation expenses, partial and targeted restrictions, with more focus on domestic producers and tourism, more access to and for international students, more flexible work arrangements, a lot of reorganizing for companies, a lot of re-training for the workforce as priorities and opportunities shift, re-examination of supply chains and company efficiency.

There will be an increase in online and home entertainment options; the limits on visitor and audience numbers will change any interactive or participative experiences such as concerts. The focus will switch to providing premium experiences so as to attract people to attend in person. Other changes in the service sector include one way pedestrian flows, contactless payments, and a decrease in interactive or touch shopping meaning maybe you won't be allowed to try clothes on anymore. These and other changes won't happen all at once, just like the virus, we will not see all of these things just vanish but many of them will decrease to the point where the question of feasibility will come into the forefront. Take tourism for instance, we will see a shift towards less populated destinations. Biometric security technologies such as face recognition might usher in easier check ins like airports with shorter lines and less person to person checks. Due to the strain the pandemic has put on the health sector, more focus will be directed here. However because of the lockdown our online presence will increase and unfortunately so will cybercrime. Already cases of credit fraud, and ransomware are becoming rampant. The increase of remote workers will require companies to reevaluate their cybersecurity to minimize security breaches while securing jobs. Don't forget automation, the pandemic speeding up the dawn of robots replacing clerical jobs. How about traffic? People trying to avoid crowded places might see a shift to more road users.

What can we do then?

Many people will be hesitant to expose themselves by shopping in person, businesses can opt to limit that by installing electronic self-opening doors and contactless payments. They might need to go beyond basic safety guidelines to ensure their clients feel safe. This might include more creative redesigning of their spaces. Restaurants may have to keep that every other seat model and to recover the cost, they might need to increase prices to remain viable. They might need to change the customer experience to justify the increase and attract those who still continue to go out. The same holds for theaters, concerts, museums and other forms of entertainment that require a certain capacity to be viable. Even offices might see a re-design with emphasis on filtration and keeping everyone safe as well as even smaller with many working from home. Sharing office equipment might decrease dramatically again due to safety and health concerns. Retail shops might need to develop better employee engagement as a better experience for clients will depend on how their employees treat them. This might take the form of better benefits like better sick leave policies, daycares, health plans and even higher wages. This might still be more cost-effective than insisting employees still go to work sick and customers seeing this and might just turn them away at some instance for good. Businesses may need to collaborate more instead of competing, teaming up to enhance customer experience and share expenses. Ever since the 80s businesses have prioritized efficiency, developing specialized suppliers from all over the globe and just-in-time manufacturing and lean HR systems. Events like the pandemic and similar to this will necessitate that companies prepare for such events therefore those who will survive are those who will put more emphasis on adaptability instead of efficiency. A crisis like this has brought forward types of leadership that do not do well like those prioritizing ego over empathy.

How to find happiness during a pandemic

COVID-19 has highlighted the physical and mental health challenges we have; however, it has also presented a great opportunity to turn it all around. How do we put it all together? Here are some habits you can adopt to find happiness and well-being in this new normal.

1. Focus on what you can do – no matter how small

With the stipulated health guideline in mind, go outside and appreciate nature. Don't be an idiot and flaunt these guidelines because you are trying to get in touch with nature. COVID-19 is real, and there's a high chance that you will get infected. Too many people have died already. Don't add to the list. Get some exercise in, relax, and enjoy the sun. Be mindful and supportive of others; you'll find that you are more flexible and accepting of what you can do with the present than you thought.

> 2. Explore the new mental toolkit – you might even help shape it

Because we have been locked indoors, we have turned to the internet to preoccupy our time. COVID-19 has brought forth a lot of attention to the wealth of resources available online. In the wake of the pandemic, let's explore and master the many opportunities we have to form meaningful social connections, practice mindfulness, self-care, virtual learning, etc. There's no time like the present to make use of the technology available to you to learn how to develop your mental health, self-reflect, exercise, develop better sleep patterns, take up a new hobby, improve skills and take care of yourself.

Practicing mindfulness, for instance, can increase our overall happiness levels as we get to live in the present, noticing and appreciating everything that's happening. We can't change the past or predict the future so there's no point in worrying about it.

However, this doesn't mean you should abandon your plans. Develop multiple contingencies and plans. Mindfulness increases our ability to be grateful, which can help adjust our attitudes and focus on what's going on in reality and not what's in our heads. Meditation amid a crisis can help you focus on what's important instead of ruminating on worrisome thoughts such as where you will get money from or what your relatives are going through. Building these habits will have a profound impact on your immune system, and if it spreads wide enough, we can tackle mental health on a global scale moving forward.

3. Empower the people around you

These are tough times, and we are all looking for support. Happy people tend to have others in mind, meaning they focus on the happiness of others rather than themselves. In this time where we are urged to take care of ourselves, taking care of others, and doing nice things for them can boost our well-being. We can take ownership of and show support to our families, communities, work, and society as a whole. A recent study reveals that the most compelling public health messages are those that focus on our collective duty to our families, friends, and communities, not just our own personal agenda. Doing random acts of kindness, donating essentials, or even money, in a time when we are all struggling can be incredibly powerful and can have a positive effect on the community and your well-being.

4. Socialize

We are social creatures, and the hardest blow COVID-19 has dealt us is denying us the opportunity to hang out with those we care about. Something we took for granted before. However, just because we have to observe social distancing doesn't mean we can't socialize. Thanks to technology, we can meet up without meeting in person. Research suggests that the act of spending time with those we love in real-time through Zoom, Skype, Google Meet, FaceTime, etc., is a really powerful way of connecting with others. By seeing their facial expressions and hearing the emotion in their voice, you are able to really connect with them.

5. We need to cope with fear and uncertainty

When the direct impact the coronavirus had on us became visible, we panicked. News of deaths, lockdown, and economic slowdown rocked the world instantly. At first, we were confused; we didn't know who to trust as contradicting information came from everywhere. This created fear and uncertainty; without a plan on how to proceed, panic ensued. People started panic buying supplies preparing for the worst; however, another kind of fear was spreading. A deeply rooted disappointment of having everything you worked so hard for be taken away from you – your livelihood and even your social freedom.

6. Smile and laugh

If anything to take away is that we all need to decompress and smile. Even laugh at our predicament. Many research shows that people who are more resilient are those that are able to smile and laugh even in the direst of their circumstances.

We have to prioritize the right things – health, happiness, family, and our well-being, because, in the end, those are the whys of our lives. They are the reason we do things. Fear and uncertainty can lead to panic; however, to move forward, we must learn from these events and become more self-aware. Rather than strive to retain the old normal, we need to find different ways to deal with the fear uncertainty creates in the new normal. By illuminating this fear with hope, we can dissipate disappointment and proactively engage with one another.

The post-COVID-19 world offers a wealth of opportunities, including a chance to dramatically change and reorganize our priorities and engagements. It has brought an emptiness to our lives; how do we deal with that? By creating healthier habits that can still find happiness and fulfillment despite everything that's happening.

Lockdown and the Environment

The coronavirus outbreak has brought how bad we have been treating our planet to the forefront. In the first months of the lockdown, cities plagued with smog reported having smog-free skies as fewer cars were on the road. Without traffic congestion and numerous cars on the road, there were fewer greenhouse gas emissions and thus no smog. For years there have been calls for climate action, for countries to pledge and commit to reducing their overall carbon emissions. However, not enough attention was being paid. Now in this pandemic, we are also facing natural disasters that are threatening our lives even more. From massively destructive hurricanes caused by the changes in weather patterns to devastating forest fires, a rise in oceanic water volumes because the polar caps are melting, resulting in floods and tsunamis. Ecosystems all over the world are getting disrupted, resulting in long winters, heatwaves, droughts, and so on, leading to the death of millions of wildlife.

This is a pretty grim picture; however, we have the chance to change things up. Despite the blows COVID-19 and nature have hit us with, they have presented us with an invaluable opportunity to redirect our energies towards things that truly matter. It has forced us to think about the things in our lives that we would like to restore and what we can do without. Given the growing concern and disastrous effects global warming has on our planet, do we really need all this commuting to work? Or all this air travel? This is the time to tackle those issues we have always been aware of but chose to ignore: climate action, dysfunctional leadership, social-economic inequality, addiction, etc. However, we must accept that this is our new reality.

We must develop a "glocal" mentality, where we think globally and act locally to make it through this. The virus has highlighted our capacity to come together and face adversity; however, we need more compassionate societies that acknowledge we are all connected despite where we live, what race we are, or how much money we earn. We have one planet; if we don't take care of it, we will face something a lot worse than the coronavirus outbreak in the future.

> *"Humankind has not woven the web of life.*
> *We are but one thread within it.*
> *Whatever we do to the web, we do to*
> *ourselves. All things are bound together.*
> *All things connect."*
>
> — Chief Seattle

REFERENCES

Bransford, J., Brown, A. L., Cocking, R. R., and National Research Council (2000). Committee on Developments in the Science of Learning. How people learn: Brain, mind, experience, and school.

Covey, S. R. (2004). The 7 habits of highly effective people: powerful lessons in personal change. New York: Simon & Schuster.

De Neve, J. E., Christakis, N. A., Fowler, J. H., and Frey, B. S. (2012). Genes, economics, and happiness. Journal of Neuroscience, Psychology, and Economics.

Dubner, Stephen J. and Levitt, Stephen D. (2007)."The Stomach-Surgery Conundrum," New York Times.

Duhigg, C. (2014). *The power of habit: why we do what we do in life and business.* New York: Random House Trade Paperbacks.

Dweck, C. S. (2007). *Mindset: the new psychology of success* (Illustrated ed.). New York: Ballantine Books.

Fuchs, E., and Flügge, G. (2014). Adult neuroplasticity: more than 40 years of research. *Neural plasticity.* https://doi.org/10.1155/2014/541870

Grupe, D. W., & Nitschke, J. B. (2013). Uncertainty and anticipation in anxiety: an integrated neurobiological and psychological perspective. *Nature reviews. Neuroscience,* 14(7), 488-501. https://doi.org/10.1038/nrn3524.

Harvard Health Publishing. (2012, March). Why behavior change is hard - and why you should keep trying. *Harvard Health.* https://www.health.harvard.edu/mind-and-mood/why-behavior-change-is-hard-and-why-you-should-keep-trying

Jebb, A. T., Tay, L., Diener, E., & Oishi, S. (2018). Happiness, income satiation and turning points around the world. *Nature Human Behaviour,* 2(1), 33–38. https://doi.org/10.1038/s41562-017-0277-0

Kahneman, D. (2010). High income improves evaluation of

life but not emotional well-being. PNAS. https://www.pnas.org/content/107/38/16489

Lanza, R., & Berman, B. (2010). Biocentrism: how life and consciousness are the keys to understanding the true nature of the universe (1st ed.). Dallas, TX: BenBella Books.

Lyubomirsky, S., Sheldon, K. M., and Schkade, D. (2005). Pursuing happiness: the architecture of sustainable change. Review of general psychology.

MIT (2019). Distinctive brain pattern helps habits form. MIT McGovern Institute. https://mcgovern.mit.edu/2018/02/08/distinctive-brain-pattern-helps-habits-form/.

McCoy, J. (2016, February 1). Fun vs. Happiness — Is There a Difference? The Healthy Mind Curriculum Blog. https://thehealthymindcurriculum.com/fun-vs-happiness-is-there-a-difference/#:%7E:text=The%20pursuit%20of%20fun%20will,sacrifice%2C%20time%20and%20sometimes%20pain.

Nelson, N., Malkoc, S., and Shiv, B. (2017). Emotions know best: the advantage of emotional versus cognitive responses to failure. J Behav Decis Mak. 31(1):40-51. doi:10.1002/bdm.2042.

Rizzo, K. M., Schiffrin, H. H., & Liss, M. (2012). Insight into the Parenthood Paradox: Mental Health Outcomes of Intensive Mothering. Journal of Child and Family Studies, 22(5), 614-620. https://doi.org/10.1007/s10826-012-9615-z

Selye, H. (1978). *The stress of life* (2nd ed.). New York: McGraw-Hill Education.

Sheldon, S., & Donahue, J. (2017). More than a feeling: Emotional cues impact the access and experience of autobiographical memories. *Memory & Cognition, 45*(5), 731–744. https://doi.org/10.3758/s13421-017-0691-6

Stoerkel, E. (2020). *Can random acts of kindness increase well-being? (Incl. 22 Ideas). PositivePsychology.Com.* https://positivepsychology.com/random-acts-kindness/.

Tan, S. Y., & Yip, A. (2018). Hans Selye (1907-1982): Founder of the stress theory. *Singapore medical journal, 59*(4), 170–171. https://doi.org/10.11622/smedj.2018043.

Tolle, E. (2005). *A new earth: awakening to your life's purpose.* London: Penguin.

Vyas, S., Even-Chen, N., Stavisky, S. D., Ryu, S. I., Nuyujukian, P., & Shenoy, K. V. (2018). Neural Population Dynamics Underlying Motor Learning Transfer. *Neuron, 97*(5), 1177-1186.e3. https://doi.org/10.1016/j.neuron.2018.01.040

Waldinger, R. (n.d.). Transcript of "What makes a good life? Lessons from the longest study on happiness". TED: Ideas worth spreading. https://www.ted.com/talks/robert_waldinger_what_makes_a_good_life_lessons_from_the_longest_study_on_happiness/transcript?referrer=playlist-what_makes_you_happy

Wagner, K. J. (1986). Diphtheria, tetanus, and pertussis: guidelines for vaccine prophylaxis and other preventive measures. The Journal of Emergency Medicine, 4(2), https://doi.org/10.1016/0736-4679(86)90092-2.

SOURCES CONSULTED

3 ways to protect your mental health during – and after – COVID-19. from https://www.weforum.org/agenda/2020/04/three-ways-to-protect-your-mental-health-from-covid-19/

3 simple hacks for building healthy habits. (2019, November 28). Psychology Today. https://www.psychologytoday.com/us/blog/functioning-flourishing/201911/3-simple-hacks-building-healthy-habits

5 reliable findings from happiness research. (n.d.). World of Psychology. https://psychcentral.com/blog/5-reliable-findings-from-happiness-research/

7 surprising benefits of failure. (2016, July 6). Wise Bread. https://www.wisebread.com/7-surprising-benefits-of-failure

8 reasons why it's so hard to really change your behavior. (2017, 22). Psychology Today. https://www.psychologytoday.com/us/blog/neuronarrative/201707/8-reasons-why-its-so-hard-really-change-your-behavior

10 Positive Psychology Studies to Change Your View of Happiness. from https://www.becomingminimalist.com/happier/

10 healthy ways to bounce back from failure. (n.d.). Verywell Mind. https://www.verywellmind.com/healthy-ways-to-cope-with-failure-4163968

A professor of happiness explains how to deal with COVID-19. from https://www.weforum.org/agenda/2020/04/coronavirus-covid19-science-of-wellbeing-yale-advice/

Believe it or not, research shows stress can make you happier (As long as it's the right kind of stress). (2018, October 25). Inc.com. https://www.inc.com/jeff-haden/believe-it-or-not-research-shows-stress-can-make-you-happier-as-long-as-its-right-kind-of-stress.html

Could money buy happiness after all? A new study thinks so - CNN. from https://www.cnn.com/2020/03/09/health/money-buys-happiness-wellness/index.html

Cohan, P. (2020, February 6). This Harvard Study of 4,000 Millionaires Revealed Something Surprising About Money and Happiness. Inc.Com. https://www.inc.com/peter-cohan/will-10-million-make-you-happier-harvard-says-yes-if-you-make-it-yourself-give-it-away.html

Dartnell, A. (2014). 6 benefits of failure that prove that it is actually a good thing. Lifehack. https://www.lifehack.org/articles/work/6-benefits-failure-that-proove-that-actually-good-thing.html

Guess what? Fear is an illusion. (2019). Thrive Global: Behavior Change Platform Reducing Employee Stress and Burnout, Enhancing Performance and Well-Being. https://thriveglobal.com/stories/guess-what-fear-is-an-illusion/

Habit formation and behavior change. (n.d.). Oxford Research Encyclopedia of Psychology. https://oxfordre.com/psychology/view/10.1093/acrefore/9780190236557.001.0001/acrefore-9780190236557-e-129

Habit formation. (n.d.). Psychology Today. https://www.psychologytoday.com/us/basics/habit-formation
Happiness | Psychology Today, from https://www.psychologytoday.com/us/basics/happiness

Hattangadi, V. (2020). *What are the four levels of happiness in life*. Dr. Vidya Hattangadi. https://drvidyahattangadi.com/what-are-the-four-levels-of-happiness-in-life/

How does valuing money affect your happiness? (n.d.). Greater Good. https://greatergood.berkeley.edu/article/item/how_does_valuing_money_affect_your_happiness

Money and happiness. (2008). Psychology Today. https://www.psychologytoday.com/us/blog/the-good-life/200806/money-and-happiness

Money and happiness: An enriching relationship? (2019, July 16). Thrive Global: Behavior Change Platform Reducing Employee Stress and Burnout, Enhancing Performance and Well-Being. https://thriveglobal.com/stories/money-and-happiness-an-enriching-relationship/

Positive Psychology: The Science of Happiness | Tal Ben-Shahar. (2018). [Video]. YouTube. https://www.youtube.com/watch?v=wBWejfLoxOA

Popova, M. (2020). *Fixed vs. growth: The two basic mindsets that shape our lives*. Brain Pickings. https://www.brainpickings.org/2014/01/29/carol-dweck-mindset/

Spending Money on Others Promotes Happiness Elizabeth

W. Dunn, from http://www.kushima.org/is/wp-content/ uploads/2014/08/Spending-Money-on-Others-Promotes-Happiness.pdf

Strong relationships, strong health. (2017). https://www. betterhealth.vic.gov.au/health/HealthyLiving/Strong-relationships-strong-health

The 3 R's of habit change: How to start new habits that actually stick. (2018). James Clear. https://jamesclear.com/ three-steps-habit-change

The circle of concern and influence. (2017). Habits for Well-being. https://www.habitsforwellbeing.com/the-circle-of-concern-and-influence/

The growth mindset - What is growth mindset - Mindset works. (n.d.). MindsetWorks | Growth Mindset | Growth Mindset Programs. https://www.mindsetworks.com/science/

The importance of learning to fail gracefully. (2016). Huff-Post. https://www.huffpost.com/entry/the-importance-of-learning-to-fail-gracefully_b_8265920

The relationship between money and happiness. (2020). The New Savvy. https://thenewsavvy.com/money-savvy/ the-relationship-between-money-and-happiness/

The Science of Happiness in Positive Psychology 101. (2020). PositivePsychology.Com. https://positivepsychology.com/happiness/

The stress of your expectations vs. reality. (n.d.). Verywell Mind. https://www.verywellmind.com/expectation-vs-reality-trap-4570968

The world counts. (n.d.). The World Counts. https://www.theworldcounts.com/happiness/four-levels-of-happiness

Webb, S. (2015). Where does happiness come from? Steven Webb. https://stevenwebb.com/where-does-happiness-come-from/Why we're unhappy -- the expectation gap | Nat Ware | TEDxKlagenfurt. (2014, November 18). [Video]. YouTube. https://www.youtube.com/watch?v=9KiUq8i9pbE

What Is Happiness and Why Is It Important? from https://positivepsychology.com/what-is-happiness/

Why is it so hard to change bad habits? (2019, March 26). Psychology Today. https://www.psychologytoday.com/us/blog/all-about-addiction/201903/why-is-it-so-hard-change-bad-habits

Why We Shouldn't Fear Failure | Psychology Today. from

https://www.psychologytoday.com/us/blog/contemporary-psychoanalysis-in-action/201703/why-we-shouldn-t-fear-failure

FINAL WORDS

How badly do you want to be happy? You may think that accepting happiness is easy, simple, and automatic, much like flipping a switch or opening a faucet. However, for most of us, happiness is a lot more elusive. We have fantasized about happiness so much that the mere notion of it triggers fear. We would, it seems, rather be unhappy and worried than try taking the risk to be happy. We are the epitome of paradox because we are nothing less than afraid to be happy.

In this book, we went through a variety of things. We defined happiness and differentiated it from other emotions and feelings. Basically, stating what happiness is and what it's not. We explored the growth mindset and how it is crucial to living a happier life, building better habits, training your brain for happiness, dealing with the fear of change, failure, stress, and a whole load of other things.

According to the Buddha, happiness and sorrow are our own responsibility, and they are completely within our control. Did you get that? *You are in control of your happiness.* Not your boss, your spouse, or your finances. YOU. So if you want to find happiness, know a big chunk of it will come from within you. *Remember that.*

> *"We are all functioning at a small fraction of our capacity to live life fully in its total meaning of loving, caring, creating and adventuring. Consequently, the actualizing of our potential can become the most exciting adventure of our lifetime."*
>
> — H. Arthur Otto

TIRED OF LIFE?

Tired of Life? by Aesop Twilight is a refreshing take on happiness like a dip in some icy water that will leave you contemplating your life choices. Why would you choose to stay miserable all this while?

Do yourself a favor and get this book. You can also subscribe to my monthly newsletter by emailing me at AesopTwilight@gmail.com to get more thrilling and engaging content. I also welcome any and all feedback.

Printed in Great Britain
by Amazon